HOW TO JITTERBUG

BY

JOHN JAVNA

WITH
CRISPIN PIERCE

DESIGNED BY
RON ADDAD & ROLAND ADDAD

DANCE PHOTOGRAPHS BY
AL STEPHENS

JITTERBUGGING BY
CRISPIN PIERCE & KELLY BUCKWALTER

St. Martin's Press   175 Fifth Avenue   New York, NY 10010

This book is dedicated to Sharon Redel and Bob Miller, with thanks for their patience and support.

ACKNOWLEDGMENTS

Thanks for making this book possible to: Crispin Pierce, Kelly Buckwalter, Al Stephens, Mary Kay Landon at KAZAN, David Gillette at Matinee, Lisa Mann for her N.Y. Jitterbug and lots more, Oz Koosed for his great Jitterbug lessons, Greg and Adrian Small, Vicki Rombs, Bob Marcus at Berkeley Music Group for the recording sessions that produced our lessons, Jim Davis for the videotape, Sas Colby for taking a chance on the Jitterbug, Buddy Schwimmer, Diana Price, Joyce Frommer, all the dancers at Determined Productions, Chuck Thompson for his Velox brainstorm, Pat McBride, Dana Walden, The Elvis Brothers, Anne Grant, Lotus, Andy Carpenter, Joann, Jenny and Peter for the dance lesson, and, of course, Ron and Roland. I didn't forget you, Linda Hogan.

THIS BOOK WAS CREATED AND PACKAGED BY
J-BIRD PRESS

CLOTHES PROVIDED BY: Matinee, 2380 Market Street, San Francisco, CA

Masquerade, 2237 Union Street, San Francisco, CA

TYPESETTING BY: KAZAN Typeset Services
PASTE-UP BY: Vicki Rombs

HOW TO JITTERBUG

Design by Ron Addad & Roland Addad
ISBN: 0-312-39574-4
Library of Congress Catalogue Number: 84-50946

First Edition
10 9 8 7 6 5 4 3 2 1

HEY, CATS AND KITTENS . . .
I'm Dr. Jitterbug with a message for YOU!
Here's your chance to learn the coolest
dance ever created. The original Rock 'n'
Roll dance. The hottest way to groove to
music since the Cavemen discovered Rhythm!

AND IT'S EASY! Anyone can learn to do
it . . . even squares. Whether you're
stuck on the King of Swing, Chuck Berry
and Elvis, or The Stray Cats, Jitterbug is
the POTION that'll SET YOU IN
MOTION! . . . Make you feel ALL REET
from your HEAD to your FEET.

Put some fun in your life, kids. Start
Jitterbuggin' TODAY!

And when they ask you how you got so
Cool, tell 'em Dr. Jitterbug sent you!

HOW TO USE THIS BOOK

1. Read over "The 5 Secrets of Jitterbug Success". All the basics of Jitterbug are here, boiled down into a few cardinal rules.
2. Listen to the record, following along on pages 14-17. It's a lesson that teaches the 2 Jitterbug Fundamentals — the Basic Step, and the Jitterbug Rhythm. Especially important for Beginners.
3. Master the Basic Step.
4. Learn the moves in order, mastering each one before you go on to the next one. This is particularly true for beginners. The reason: a lot of moves are built on previous moves. You have to know the Hand-Change, for example, before you can do the Shoulder-Slide.
5. If you don't want to do it my way, make up your own. Have fun.

HOW TO LEARN A MOVE:

1. Read the instructions through. Try to get a feel for the general movement being described. Don't pay too much attention to details at first. Study the photos.
2. When you've got an idea of what you're going to be doing, follow the instructions step-by-step, moving through them very slowly. No music yet. Concentrate on arm movement and body placement first. Then get the footwork down.
3. Now try it all together: body, arms, feet, to the correct rhythm. Still no music yet.
4. Music time. Get a slow tune like *Calendar Girl*, by Neal Sedaka, or *Isn't She Lovely,* by Stevie Wonder, and practice the move until you've got it down.
5. Speed up the music. Elvis' *All Shook Up* is my favorite for this stage.

EACH NEW MOVE IS PRESENTED IN AN EASY-TO-FOLLOW, STANDARD FORMAT:

Introduces a move, tells you a few vital facts.

Lettered photos show you what the move looks like.

The move is broken up into "Motions". This line identifies what photos correspond to the specific instruction.

The actual instruction. Remember: they're describing BODY MOVEMENT, and are meant to be FOLLOWED, not just read. Don't try too hard to understand them without MOVING too.

HOW TO JITTERBUG
CONTENTS

THE FIVE SECRETS OF
JITTERBUG SUCCESS

SECRET #1 — HAVE FUN!!

There's only one reason to learn Jitterbug — TO HAVE FUN. No matter how good (or not so good) you are, no matter how much time you spend learning the moves in this book, having fun should always be your main motivation.

If you start Jitterbugging in public, you'll find that a lot of people take this dance very seriously. That's fine — experts are wonderful to watch, and they're an inspiration to beginners. But no one should ever get so wrapped up in getting the moves right that they stop enjoying them. Don't let someone else's abilities make you competitive or self-conscious. You know you're doing fine if you and your partner have a good time together.

So why bother WORKING at getting the steps down pat? Two good reasons. First, knowing the steps gives you the freedom to really enjoy yourself. If you don't have to concentrate all the time on what your feet are supposed to be doing, you can get into the music more; you can feel the energy and excitement in your own movement. And second, the more you know, the more interesting the dance is. When you add new moves to your repertoire, you can start to play with different combinations of them — and ultimately, you create your own dance!

So relax. Get a partner you really dig. Put on some music you love. And start practicing. Soon "slow, slow, quick-quick" will turn into "Wow! That's a gas!" And that's the way it should be. Fun.

THE FIVE SECRETS OF
JITTERBUG SUCCESS

SECRET #2 — WATCH YOUR WEIGHT

One thing you've always got to be aware of while you're learning to dance is where your weight is. I don't mean the effect of a diet, or where you stashed your barbells. I mean which foot you're putting your weight on.

Look at the picture. Can you tell which foot Crispin and Kelly each have their weight on? If not, put the book down quietly and take up ping pong.

As you read and run through the instructions, be conscious of where your weight is supposed to be, and how it changes from step to step. There are two simple rules that you should remember:

1) When stepping, always put your weight on the leading foot (the one you've stepped with).

2) Step onto the BALL of your foot. Watch out for GODZILLA FEET. Dance instructors worry that people who learn to dance from a book will interpret the instruction to "step" as an invitation to imitate Godzilla, stomping around the dance floor like a 40-ton prehistoric monster. When you change weight, don't plunk your feet down as if they were made of lead. Keep your weight in the front, on the balls of your feet.

Dance is a smooth motion, and your steps should be smooth and light. If your weight is placed incorrectly, your whole body will be out of position. You won't be in place for your next step, and the move won't work. Plus, you'll throw your partner off. If you're having trouble with a move, it may be because you've got your weight in the wrong place.

THE FIVE SECRETS OF
JITTERBUG SUCCESS

YOU'D NEVER KNOW

SECRET #3 — KEEP THE BEAT

You have to keep an even beat with your feet when you dance. In Jitterbug, this isn't as simple as it sounds. A lot of people kind of stumble (or run) through a fancy move, oblivious to rhythm or tempo, and then have to pause to get the beat again before continuing to dance.

The best way to assure that you'll be dancing to the beat is to get the rhythm correct right from the beginning, when you're first learning the moves. That means paying attention to the "count" at the end of each "motion" in the instructions. This tells you how many beats there are for each movement.

THE STANDARD JITTERBUG RHYTHM:

There are six beats to most Jitterbug moves. As you learn the steps, you should count these beats out loud.

You go: "Slow, slow, quick-quick".

That doesn't look like six beats, does it? It looks like four. But here's the secret: you hold each "slow" for two beats, and each "quick" for one.

An easy way to understand it: look at a clock with a second-hand. For the first two seconds, you say "slow". For the third and fourth seconds you say "slow" again. And then you say "quick" for each of the fifth and sixth seconds. So for a six-second count, you say "slow, slow, quick-quick". That's the rhythm to which you'll be moving your feet. Eventually it'll become second nature, and you won't have to think about it when you dance. To start, though, you should pay particular attention to it.

At the beginning, you should use six seconds for a full count. Later, when you really start dancing, you'll cut it down to about three — one second for each "slow", and a half-second for each "quick".

Learning this rhythm is so important that I've included it on the free record. Be sure to listen to it.

Other tips:
- When you start a dance, take the time to listen for the beat before you begin.
- You can pick out the beat of a song by keeping an ear to the drums.
- Some moves are four beats instead of six. They are learned as "quick-quick-quick-quick", and are usually turns. The "count" will tell you which they are.

"I'm a Success after 40"

That's his fifth drink. I wonder if he can still dance.

THE FIVE SECRETS OF
JITTERBUG SUCCESS

SECRET #4 — LEARN TO LEAD, LEARN TO FOLLOW

In Jitterbug, there's a leader and a follower. This relationship is clearly defined, and very important. Since the couple is moving TOGETHER, they can't *both* decide which direction in which to go, or which move to do. That would be total confusion and would look terrible. So there's an "official" decider. Traditionally, in Jitterbug, the man is the leader, so that's how it's designated here.

Good leading and good following are equally difficult, because the communication between dancers is very subtle. There's no time to stop and discuss what comes next when you're really moving. The leader has to know how to tell his partner what to do, using his hands and body, and the follower has to understand what he's telling her. It has to be done smoothly. A leader who yanks or tugs his partner in the direction he wants her to go, or who doesn't let her know what to expect, is a lousy dance partner. On the other hand, a follower who doesn't respond to a lead, or who fights her partner's leads, is also a poor dancer.

All in all, this might be the hardest part of Jitterbugging. Keep trying and eventually you'll master it. A tip: don't be afraid to ask your partner what you're doing right or wrong. Your partner knows first-hand what your strengths and weaknesses are.

HERE'S WHAT THE LEADER DOES:
- Always starts with the Basic Step
- Always starts with his left foot
- Starts slow and steady with a new partner
- Gets the couple started on the right rhythm and maintains it
- Decides what steps or moves the couple's going to do (think ahead as you dance, so you know what comes next)
- Communicates the moves clearly and smoothly to his partner and GENTLY guides her
- Keeps things under control — if couple starts to get too far apart, or out of synch, etc., he brings them back and keeps the tempo even and relaxed
- Stays within his limits. If you haven't mastered a move, how can you expect your partner to?
- Makes sure they don't smash into things or people as they dance

HERE'S WHAT THE FOLLOWER DOES:
- Never attempts to take the lead; instant chaos
- Never anticipates partner's lead
- Watches for signals or gestures that tell what they're doing next
- Keeps tension in arms so she can feel the leads as they're given
- Always steps with right foot first
- Compensates, if possible, for poor leads (unfortunately, a frequent problem)
- Lets partner guide her through moves that are not familiar to her

BOTH LEADER AND FOLLOWER:
- Must know their parts before they try dancing
- Will find it helpful to practice alone, as if they've got a partner
- Should maintain a slight pressure through the arms and hands as they dance
- Should try to keep going if they make a mistake

"It's high time you learned the facts of life, George!"

THE FIVE SECRETS OF
JITTERBUG SUCCESS

SECRET #5 — COMMUNICATE WITH YOUR PARTNER

There are two types of communication. One relates to Leading and Following. The other is common sense. Both will make you a better dancer.

1) **COMMUNICATING THE MOVES.** Each move has a distinct motion, as it begins, that a leader uses as a signal to tell a follower what they're going to do. The man should be sure he gives this signal clearly, and the woman should be on the lookout for it. As you learn the moves, carefully identify the signals for each one. An example: In the Shoulder Slide, the man steps forward and raises his arms in a sweeping motion. This gesture is unique to this move, and the woman should automatically recognize it . . . IF the man gives it properly! You can see that it's important for the man to give the signal as early as possible, too — since the woman has to wait for it before she can take HER step.

2) **THERE'S A SPECIAL KIND OF COMMUNICATION** that two people have when they're really doing something TOGETHER. You can feel it when it's happening. And frankly, no matter how many fancy moves you do, if you can achieve this with your partner, you're getting the most out of dancing. Moving *together* is the key. A couple that moves smoothly together will out-dance the fancy-pants every time. In most modern dancing, people don't even look at each other. They don't touch. They don't really even need a partner. Jitterbug is different, and you'll enjoy the difference if you take advantage of it.

OTHER TIPS:

- The Hands: most of the "talking" you do with your partner will be with your hands. You communicate rhythm, direction, energy . . . and a lot more through your hands. Try closing your eyes while you dance and you'll understand.

- The Voice: Forget the rules — there's no reason why you can't talk to your partner while you dance — about the moves, about the music . . . whatever you want. You can even tell your partner what move you want to do next. Why not? One caution: it's really a drag if your partner starts giving instructions or counting for you while you dance.

- The Eyes: I don't know why, but many dancers seem to avoid each other's eyes while they dance. It's fun to look into your partner's eyes. Try it.

He's So Sensitive

BEGINNING

The beginning moves are the foundation to all your Jitterbugging, so you should take the time to master them. But relax and enjoy yourself while you learn. Don't rush through the moves — take them slowly, one at a time. If you get stuck on a move, let it go for a while and come back to it later. And if you make mistakes, it's no big deal — everyone does when they're starting out.

The main thing is to keep at it and have fun!

The 1948 Trav-ler Electric Phonograph

BE A JITTERBUG
CLOTHES MAKE THE JITTERBUG

Try Dr. Jitterbug's Extra-Strength Motion Potion

A Jitterbug always looks sharp, because a Jitterbug knows that dancing isn't just knowing the steps — style counts too. You can look like a great dancer without ever getting out of your seat IF you've got the right threads on. So your first Jitterbug lesson is what to wear. Here are Jitterbug outfits that'll make you look like a Cool Cat on the dance floor.

THE HEPCAT (The 40s Mr. Cool)

Wide-brimmed hat (remove when dancing).

Padded shoulders.

Loud, wide tie. The louder and wider, the better.

Never close your hands unless you're snapping your fingers.

Double-breasted jacket. Length: Almost to knees.

Never stand with both feet on the ground — perch on one foot. This is also the Hepcat's natural walk.

Baggy floor-length pants (doubles as a sleeping bag if your car breaks down in the middle of nowhere on the way home from a dance).

White shoes or Wing Tips.

THE GREASER

Grease hair back. Apply liberally. If necessary, use baby oil, but never use Crisco — it attracts flies.

Cool shades Remove only when dancing.

Do not smile. Sneer whenever possible.

Roll sleeves up. Good place to keep a cigarette pack too.

Hold your breath. Exhale only if absolutely necessary, and only if no one's watching.

If you don't have a tattoo, use a felt-tip marker to paint one on.

Clean white T-shirt for formal occasions.

Black leather jacket.

NEVER wear designer jeans. Roll up pants so sox are visible.

Roach Stompers (pointed toes are particularly good for squashing bugs in hard-to-reach corners).

White socks.

BEGINNING
OPEN POSITION

Hey — that doesn't look too hard!

This is the basic position you'll use for Jitterbug. To begin, stand with your feet about 6" apart, a foot from your partner. Elbows are bent loosely, with hands held at about waist-height. Weight is evenly on both feet. Keep some tension in your arms — don't let them droop.

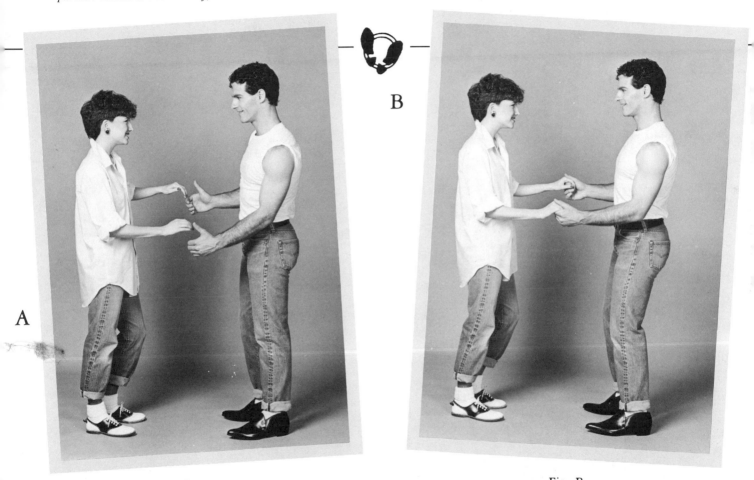

B

A

Fig. A

· Face each other, standing about a foot apart.
MEN:
· Curl your fingers slightly and stick your thumbs in the air like The Fonz.

WOMEN:
· Curl your hands slightly, palms facing down, fingers together, as in the "dog paddle".

Fig. B

WOMEN:
· Place your hands on top of his fingers, with fingertips touching his palms inside the "curl", thumb outside, resting on the top of his fingers.

MEN:
· Gently close your thumb down on top of her knuckles.
HOLD HANDS COMFORTABLY:
· Not too tight, but tight enough so they don't come apart.

Spin your latest Jitterbug 45s on this 1952 RCA Victrola

BEGINNING • MOVE 1
BASIC STEP

The ultimate Jitterbug men's footwear — 2-tone Wingtips

The Jitterbug is built around this step, so take your time and master it COMPLETELY before going on to others. It's four simple motions: a step to the side, a step to the other side, a step back, and a step forward. But of course you've got to do it to music, so you need a steady rhythm. Use what you learned on p. 8 *and listen to the lesson on the enclosed record to get the Jitterbug Rhythm (the "Count") down pat on this move!*

We've given each motion of the Basic Step an entire page. A more advanced version of the Basic is included in the Intermediate Section.

A

STYLE POINTERS
Here's what the move looks like alone. Practice by yourself in front of a mirror to get the feel of it. The key is to keep it smooth — don't be jerky, and don't lunge (a 6" step is easy to control, a 16" step isn't). And . . . you're not auditioning for the role of the Frankenstein monster, so don't STOMP, step!! You're dancing, not putting out fires with your feet!

Dr. Jitterbug sez: A gal can ask a guy to dance IF she does it the right way.

WRONG
"If you're not doing anything, would you mind dancing with me?"

RIGHT
"Your dream girl has arrived, you hunk. Let's dance!"

FIRST MOTION — Fig. A

MEN:
Step 6" to left with your left foot.
WOMEN:
Step 6" to right with your right foot.
AS YOU STEP:
Le—e—ean into the step

pushing off opposite foot.
Dip your shoulder.
Bend your knee slightly.
AS FOOT LANDS:
Transfer weight to the ball of it.
Point toe out diagonally.
COUNT:
"Slow" (2 beats)

BASIC STEP

Watch your date's eyes pop out when you pick her up in this 1954 Dodge

"Why Didn't I Do This Before!"

B

STYLE POINTERS

This is what it looks like alone. Again, practice it in front of a mirror. Combine it with the first move for a continuous side-to-side motion.
NOTE: the reason you step in place in the second motion (instead of stepping out) is to keep your legs from getting too far apart. That's something to remember and watch out for. It messes up your dancing if your steps are too big, or legs spread too wide.

Getting in the groove for the Big Dance

SECOND MOTION — Fig. B

Essentially the reverse of the First Motion, but instead of stepping OUT 6", you step in place with the opposite foot
MEN:
· Lift your right foot a few inches, then put it back down toe-to-heel, with weight on the ball of foot
WOMEN:

· Lift your left foot a few inches, then put it back down toe-to-heel, with weight on the ball of foot
· REPEAT ALL OTHER DETAILS OF THE FIRST MOTION
COUNT:
· "Slow" (2 beats)

Dig it! American Bandstand is on in 15 minutes!

BEGINNING • MOVE 1
BASIC STEP

The last two motions in the Basic Step are a little harder to learn than the first two, so you'll have to concentrate a bit more. It's not exactly right to call them separate motions — they're really one continuous motion with two distinct parts. Together, they're called the "Rock-Step", because you "rock" back with one foot, then "step" forward with the other. The movement is like a rocking horse — you move away from your partner and move towards your partner in one smooth move.

The count on this is "quick-quick", or 1 count for each motion, whereas the first two moves both have two counts for each motion.

C

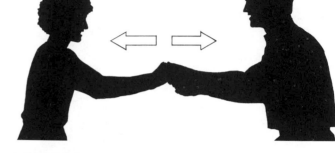

IMPORTANT TIP

Just before you step back, give your partner a little shove with your arms. Most beginners leave their arms limp (see Spaghetti Arms, p. 26) or pull away from their partners as they rock back. But if you keep your arms tight and PUSH as you begin your "rock", you add to the communication with your partner. An exercise to get the feel of the push: Do the step in front of a wall. As you rock back, gently push the wall. That's the resistance you want to feel from your partner, and should provide as well.

THIRD MOTION — THE "ROCK" — Fig. C

MAN:
Push off your right foot, stepping back about 6″ with your left.
WOMAN:
Push off your left foot, stepping back about 6″ with your right.
AS FOOT LANDS:
Put all weight on ball of your rear foot, bending your knee slightly as you do.
· Your back heel never touches the floor.
· Lift your front foot about 3″ off floor.
· Keep your elbows bent. If your arms are straight, you're too far away from each other.
COUNT:
· "Quick" (1 beat)

Close-up of the feet in the "Rock" position

"Jitterbug Saturday night? You bet!"

IMPORTANT TIP:
From the Fourth Motion, you go directly back to the First Motion. You DO NOT bring your feet together after the Fourth Motion (the "Step")

D

Close-up of the feet in the "Step" position

FOURTH MOTION — THE "STEP" — Fig. D

MEN and WOMEN:
· Push yourself forward by pushing OFF your rear foot, simultaneously lowering front foot (that's the "Step")
AS YOU STEP:
· Lean towards your partner (but keep your balance).
· Keep your elbows bent, tucked into your body.

· Your hands are up, just below the shoulders.
AS FRONT FOOT LANDS:
· Put all weight on the ball of it. Pick your rear heel off the floor; no weight on your rear foot.
COUNT:
· "Quick" (1 beat)

EXCERCISE
The whole "Rock-Step" is similar to the rocking of a rocking horse. Back and forward, away from your partner and toward your partner. Try putting one foot back 6", and rocking like a rocking horse by alternately pushing and pulling your partner.

ONE-HAND LEAD

Now that you know the Basic Step, here are two variations you can add that will change the LOOK of the dance without really changing what you're doing. A TIP: Using small variations like *these sometimes makes the difference between looking SHARP and Dullsville. As you go through the book, think of your own.*

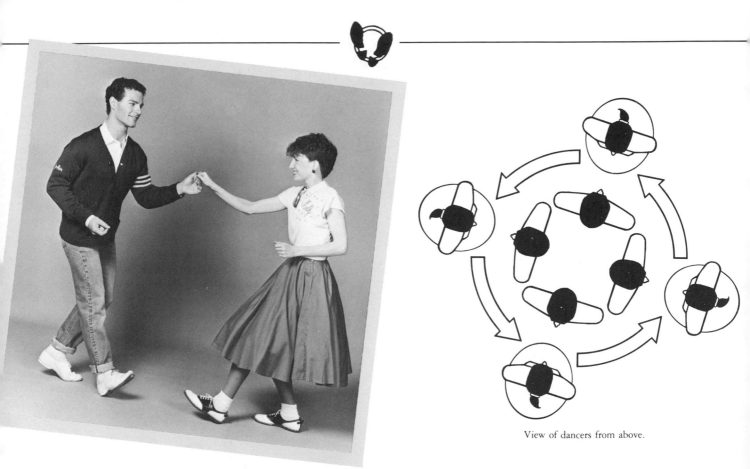

View of dancers from above.

You've probably seen movies of Jitterbuggers holding only one of their partner's hands as they dance. This is a simple variation of the Basic Step in Open Position.

TO DO IT:

After a "rock-step", the man simply lets go of the woman's left hand with his right hand and they keep on doing the Basic, holding just one hand. (When you get to the "rock-step", tighten your grip a little, and don't forget the push-off. It's even more important when you're only holding one hand.)

To get back to Open Position, man holds out his right hand and woman responds by holding out her left hand. Man takes it and they keep on dancing.

ANOTHER VARIATION

As you do the Basic Step, try making a circle around the floor. You accomplish this by stepping farther out on your first step after the "rock-step" (man's left foot, woman's right) than you normally would. After 4 Basics, you should wind up in the same place you started.

WARNING **WARNING**

WATCH OUT FOR SPAGHETTI ARMS:

One of the most common maladies among female Jitterbuggers is Spaghetti Arms — loose, limp arms that hang like wet spaghetti when a woman dances.

And most of them don't even realize they're doing it! Don't ignore the problem — catch it now! Keep tension in your arms when you're dancing.

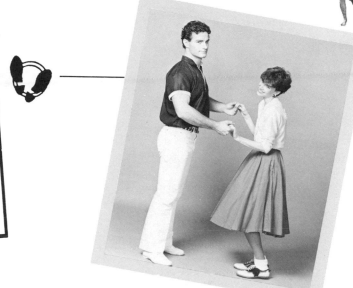

A woman with Spaghetti Arms can't follow her partner's leads.

IN THE NEXT FEW PAGES, YOU'LL BE INTRODUCED TO SOME SIMPLE TURNS. THERE ARE TWO THINGS YOU SHOULD KNOW TO HELP YOU LEARN THEM:

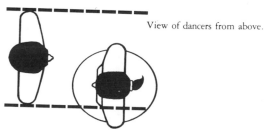

View of dancers from above.

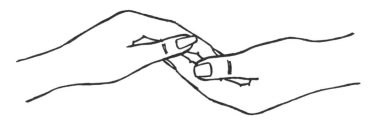

1) PASSING POSITION. For any move in which the partners will walk past each other, the man sets himself up a little to the left or right of his partner (depending on which side they'll be passing on). The couple is still standing face-to-face, but with a slight shading to one side this makes it possible for both partners to move straight ahead without crashing into each other.

2) WHEN TURNING, USE "PALM-TO-PALM" CONTACT. If you maintain the standard grip (p. 13) when you turn, someone's going to wind up with a broken wrist. The solution: as you begin to turn, you open your hands and rotate them so that each of you has your fingertips in your partner's palm. When you're done with the turn, you rotate them back into the standard grip.

"Take two Underarm Turns and call me in the morning"

BEGINNING • MOVE 3
UNDERARM TURN

In this classic move, the idea is simple: you trade places with your partner by walking forward past each other, turning to face each other, and then doing the "rock-step". The hardest part of the move is mastering the footwork so you "rock-step" at the proper time. Work on it.

Count is "slow, slow, quick-quick" while you're learning. Later, you can try it as a 4-beat move ("quick-quick-quick-quick"). Either way is fine.

TO START: Complete a Basic Step. Your first step out of the "rock-step" is the first step of this move.

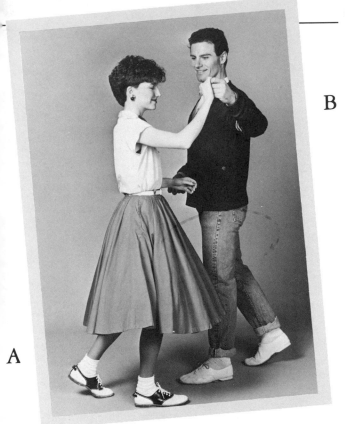

A

B

C

FIRST MOTION — Fig. A

MEN:
· Raise left hand, making an arch in front of partner with your left and her right arm.
· Begin to walk past her: step forward 6″ onto the ball of your left foot, passing her on YOUR left.

WOMEN:
· Begin to walk past partner: step forward 6″ onto ball of right foot, under the arch, passing him on YOUR left.

AS YOU STEP:
· Man releases woman's left hand with his right.
· Transfer weight to ball of man's left, woman's right foot.
· COUNT: "Slow" (2 beats)

SECOND MOTION — Figs. B & C

MEN:
· Step forward and around to the left with your right foot, until you face your partner.

WOMEN:
· Begin a step with your left foot: Use the momentum of the step to spin to your right on the ball of your right foot until you face your partner. USE PALM-TO-PALM CONTACT TO ALLOW YOU TO TURN

WITHOUT BREAKING YOUR WRISTS!!

AS FOOT LANDS:
· Put weight on ball of man's right and woman's left foot.
· Partners are facing each other, ready to "rock" back.
· Arms are about chest-high, elbows bent, with loose hand-grip.
· COUNT: "Slow" (2 beats)

Wow. Jitterbug sure is MY cup of tea.

Hot Dog! It's Basie's "One O'Clock Jump!"

E

D

THIRD MOTION — The "Rock" — Fig. D

MEN:
· Step back with left foot, into "rock" position.

WOMEN:
· Step back with right foot, into "rock" position.
· COUNT: "Quick" (1 beat).

AS IN THE 1-HAND LEAD, GET A FIRM GRIP WITH YOUR HAND AND GIVE PARTNER A SMOOTH PUSH AS YOU "ROCK" BACK

FOURTH MOTION — The "Step" — Fig. E

MEN:
· As you complete the "rock-step", hold your free hand out and catch your partner's left hand so you are back in Open Position.

WOMEN:
· When he holds his hand out, that's the signal you're going back into open position. Hold your left hand out to him.
· COUNT: "Quick" (1 beat).

AS YOU BEGIN THE BASIC STEP, YOU WILL HAVE TO ROTATE MAN'S LEFT, WOMAN'S RIGHT HAND TO GET BACK TO OPEN POSITION HAND-GRIP

BEGINNING • MOVE 4
REVERSE UNDERARM TURN

This is an option after the Underarm Turn. Instead of going back to the Basic Step, you do a second underarm turn in the opposite direction, going back to your original position. So, beginning with your first Basic: you do a Basic, you switch places in an Underarm Turn, you switch places AGAIN in a Reverse Underarm Turn, and then do a Basic Step. The move starts at the "step" after the Underarm Turn.

A

B

AS YOU COMPLETE THE "ROCK-STEP" AFTER THE UNDERARM TURN — Fig. A

· The man raises his left arm (forearm across forehead), and the woman raises her right arm (forearm vertical, elbow down), making a window with partner's arm. LOOK AT EACH OTHER THROUGH THE WINDOW (Make it big enough to see each other through).

FIRST MOTION — Fig. B

MEN:
· Place the window over your partner's head as you step forward and around her with your left foot. PASS HER ON YOUR RIGHT.
WOMEN:
· Begin to turn left, pivoting on your left foot as you step forward with your right, under the "window".
AS FOOT LANDS:
· Transfer weight to ball of it.
· COUNT: "Slow" (2 beats).

REVERSE UNDERARM TURN

It's All History —but No Dates!

This weekend will be heaven

2

C

D

SECOND MOTION — Fig. C

MEN:
- Step forward and around your partner with your right foot, beginning to turn to face her and continuing to turn her until she faces you.

WOMEN:
- Turn completely around to face your partner by pivoting on your right foot as you step back with your left.

AS FOOT LANDS:
- Transfer weight to ball of it.
- COUNT: "Slow" (2 beats).

THIRD MOTION — The "Rock" — Fig. D

MEN:
- Pivot on your right foot to face your partner, stepping back into the "rock" position with your left foot.

WOMEN:
- Step back with your right foot into the "rock".
- COUNT: "Quick" (1 beat).

- NOW COMPLETE THE "ROCK-STEP" WITH THE "STEP", AND GO BACK INTO A BASIC STEP.

BEGINNING • MOVE 5
HAND-CHANGE

This is a variation of the Underarm Turn. It looks cool, and it's a very important building block for other Jitterbug moves. You learn two skills you'll use frequently: 1) How to change hands while dancing, and 2) What to do AFTER you've changed hands. It's a little harder than the previous moves, but you need to master it. It starts as you complete the Reverse Underarm Turn.

A

B

C

TO START — Figs. A & B

· AS YOU BEGIN THE "ROCK-STEP" AFTER A REVERSE UNDERARM TURN:
· Before straightening your arms to "rock" back (fig. C, p. 22), man places woman's right hand into his right hand (DON'T throw it). Then couple completes the "rock-step" holding right hand to right hand·

SECOND MOTION — Fig. C

MEN:
· Raise right arm to right side, making an arch in front of partner with her right arm.
· Step forward with left foot, passing her on YOUR right.

WOMEN:
· Bring right arm in towards you and across your chest (right hand by left ear), making an arch in front of you with man's right arm.
· Pivot to left as you step forward with right foot, under arch.

AS FOOT LANDS:
· Transfer weight to ball of it.
· Woman is under arch.
· COUNT: "Slow" (2 beats).

Since I learned to Jitterbug, I'm the most popular girl in town

RELIEF!

D

E

F

THIRD MOTION — Figs. D & E

MEN:
- Step forward with right foot, pivoting to the left so you're facing sideways, with both feet pointing left.
- As you step, bring right arm over woman's head and place her right hand into your left, behind your back (DON'T throw it).

WOMEN:
- Turn completely around to to face your partner by pivoting on your right foot as you step back with your left.

AS FOOT LANDS:
- Transfer weight to ball of it.
- Man's left, woman's right hand are palm-to-palm behind his back.
- Woman faces man's side.
- COUNT: "Slow" (2 beats).

FOURTH MOTION — The "Rock" — Fig. F

MEN:
- Pivot counter-clockwise on the ball of your right foot, stepping back with your left into "rock" position to face your partner.

WOMEN:
- Step back with right foot into "rock" position.

AS FOOT LANDS:
- Transfer weight to ball of it.
- Arms are extended.
- COUNT: "Quick" (1 beat).
COMPLETE "ROCK-STEP" AND RETURN TO BASIC STEP.

SPEEDY

BEGINNING • MOVE 6
FORWARD PASS

Here's another way to exchange places while dancing. This time, though, you don't need any "arches" or "windows" — you let go of your partner's hand and spin PAST each other. Woman must have

tension in her arm to respond to the man's lead. The move begins out of a 1-Hand Lead, or any turn that leaves you holding one hand.

If only I'd learned to Jitterbug, she'd be MY girl now!

What's going on here? Where are the regular models?

I told them a reporter from *Time* magazine wanted to talk to them on the phone about the Jitterbug revival. They fell for it like a ton of bricks!

This is our Big Chance!

I'm not even getting paid for this.

A

B

C

As you complete the "rock-step" in a 1-Hand Lead (or after an Underarm Turn or a Hand-Change):
Man smoothly pulls woman's right hand towards him and across past his right shoulder. When hand is as far right as it will go, man lets go of her hand. Weight is on ball of man's

right & woman's left foot.

Man steps forward with left foot, passing woman on HIS right. At the same time, woman steps forward with her right foot, passing him on HER right. Weight is on man's left, woman's right foot.

Man steps with right foot,

pivoting counter-clockwise on ball of left foot to face partner. Woman pivots counter-clockwise on ball of right foot, stepping back with left foot to face partner.

As they turn to face each other, they catch hands

They "rock-step" in a 1-Hand Lead.

NOTE: Woman must have tension in her arm to make this turn effective. Spaghetti Arms will ruin the move.

TEEN SCENE

Jitterbug
Romance:
The First Date

I'M AFRAID__ER__ COULD YOU TRUST ME FOR THE MEAL?

Are you in the know?

The lathered lady is —
- ☐ Brushing up on beauty
- ☐ Banishing 5 o'clock shadow
- ☐ A little shaver

If stranded on a dance floor, should you —
- ☐ Join the wallflowers
- ☐ Retreat to the dressing-room
- ☐ Yoo-hoo to the stag line

Are you in the know?

Which gal would you ask to complete a foursome?
☐ A Suave Sally ☐ A numb number ☐ A character from the carnival

TRUE OR FALSE?

JITTERBUGGING IS PERFECTLY OKAY DURING "THOSE CERTAIN DAYS"

If you're conversation-shy in a crowd, what helps overcome it?
☐ Take a public-speaking course   ☐ Avoid gang gatherings   ☐ Go in for sports

TEEN TIPS

Here's a trick if you've got an extra pair of saddle shoes, girls: paint them in your school colors, and you'll have a real eye-catcher at the next football game or sock hop!

"Now that I've learned to Jitter-bug, can we go steady?"

CLOSED POSITION

EYES FOCUS ON YOUR *Legs!*

This is a classic for the Lindy and Jitterbug, but a little harder to do well than the Open Position because you're literally moving together. It's a MUST for all dancers. First get the stance right, and get comfortable in it. Then practice the Basic in it. NOTE: It's fun to exaggerate the motions in Closed Position, dipping really low & posing as you step back.

B

C

CLOSED POSITION— Fig. A

- Man and woman face each other, slightly in "V" position — i.e., man's right side and woman's left side are closer together than man's left and woman's right.
- Woman places her left hand on man's shoulder.
- Man places his right hand on her shoulder blade or back, depending on what's most comfortable.
- GRIP: Woman holds her right hand out, palm down, fingers slightly curled. Man reaches his left hand over hers so his thumb is diagonally across the back of her fingers, and wraps his fingers around her hand so they are touching the inside of it.

BASIC STEP IN CLOSED POSITION— Figs. B & C

- First and Second Motions are identical to Basic in Open Position (Figs. B & C).

BEGINNING • MOVE 7
CLOSED POSITION

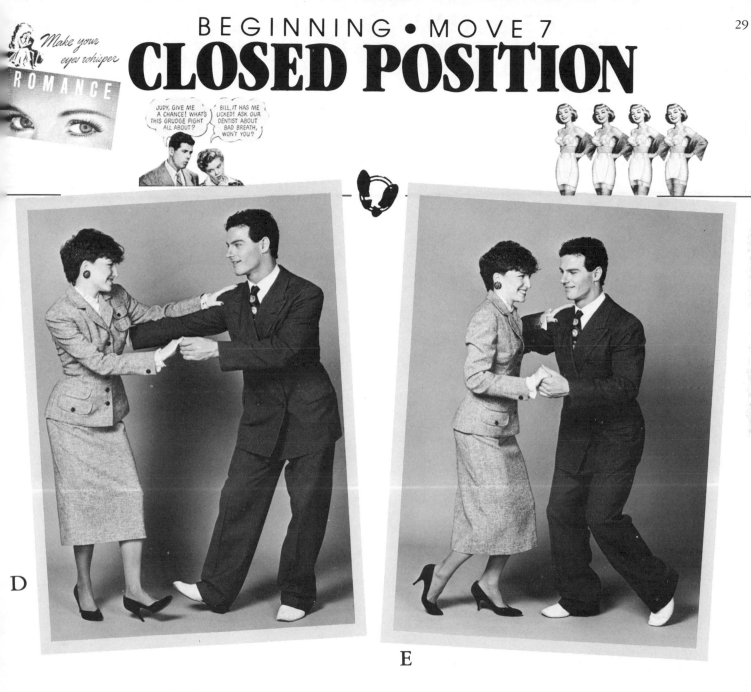

D

E

Fig. D

· The "Rock-Step" is slightly different:
On the "Rock", the couple opens up the stance, stepping away from each other as they "rock" back (Fig. D).

Fig. E

· On the "step", they come back toward each other, bending the front knee slightly (Fig. E).

BEGINNING • MOVE 8
CLOSED TO OPEN

You have to learn to switch smoothly between Open and Closed Position as you dance, since they're equally important. Make sure you know the Closed Position well before trying to switch to Open.

Practice slowly at first, doing a Basic, a Switch, a Basic, a Switch, etc. NOTE: Switching from Closed to Open is the harder of the two, since it involves an Underarm Turn. Open to Closed should be easy.

A

B

- To go from the Closed Position to the Open Position, you begin the change on the "rock-step". Man makes up his mind on the "rock", because he begins a turn on the "step" if he's switching to Open Position.

- On "step", man begins to raise left hand, making an arch with his left and woman's right arm. He exerts light pressure on her back in the direction of the arch to guide her under it.

- On First Motion, man guides woman under arch as he steps with his left foot, and she steps forward with her right.

- From then on, it's an Underarm Turn.

BEGINNING • MOVE 8
OPEN TO CLOSED

Betty's Wretched

Dr. Jitterbug sez:
Don't be left out!
Learn to Jitterbug
today!

"Well, son, it's
time I told you the
facts of Jitterbug"

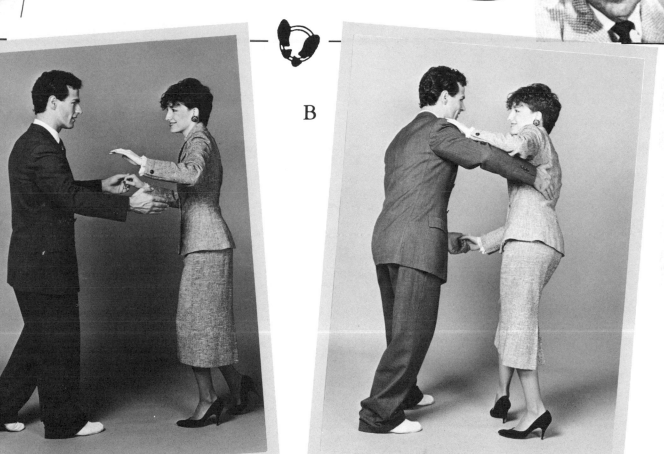

A

B

· To get from Open Position to Closed Position, you begin the change on the "rock-step". Man makes up his mind on the "rock", because the change begins on the "step".

· Out of a Basic or a turn of any kind, the man smoothly pulls the woman toward him on the "step" (releasing her left hand with his right if they're doing a Basic in Open Position) and slides his hand around onto her back. When she feels him doing this, she puts her hand on his shoulder, and they rotate their other hands around to the Closed Position grip.

· They proceed into a Closed Position Basic without missing a beat.

BEGINNING ROUTINE

Now that you've learned the Beginning Moves, it's time to put them together into a dance. This is a SAMPLE Routine — one of the many ways you can combine the moves into a sequence. It starts and ends in the Open Position, so you can keep repeating it if you want. After you've mastered it, try adding your own variations to it.

Try it without music first (you can do it to any song) to see if you know the moves well enough. Then add some slow music, speeding the music up as you get better at it.

Even if you know the moves, the difficult part at this stage is the TRANSITION from one move to another. You'll find that the key to this is beginning the transition on the "STEP" of the "rock-step" BEFORE each move. Have fun!

---

1. Basic Step in Open Position "Slow, slow, quick, quick"

TRANSITION: Your first step forward after the "rock-step" is the First Motion of the next Basic Step.

2. Basic Step in Open Position "Slow, slow, quick, quick"

TRANSITION: As you "rock-step", man assumes passing position (left side to left side). On the "step", he begins to raise his left arm (and woman's right), making an arch in front of the woman.

3. Underarm Turn "Slow, slow, quick, quick"

TRANSITION: As you do the "step" in the "rock-step", man raises his left arm (forearm across forehead) and woman's right, making a window. Look at each other through the window.

4. Reverse Underarm Turn

TRANSITION: As you face each other after a Reverse Underarm Turn, you are holding one hand (man's left, woman's right).

5. Basic Step in One-Hand Lead "Slow, slow, quick, quick"

6. Basic Step in One-Hand Lead "Slow, slow, quick, quick"

TRANSITION: As you "step" in the "rock-step", man smoothly begins to pull woman's right hand across to his right shoulder, beginning their forward motion.

7. Forward Pass

"Slow, slow, quick, quick"

TRANSITION: Man catches woman's right hand with his right hand as you turn to face each other. You are in a Hand-Change position on the "rock-step".

8. Behind-the-Back Hand-Change

"Slow, slow, quick, quick"

TRANSITION: As you do the "step" in the "rock-step", man smoothly pulls the woman towards him, sliding his right hand around her, placing it on her back. She responds by putting her left hand on his shoulder.

9. Basic Step in Closed Position

"Slow, slow, quick, quick"

10. Basic Step in Closed Position

"Slow, slow, quick, quick"

TRANSITION: On "step" of "rock-step", man raises his left arm (woman's right) in an arch, and gently begins to guide her under the arch, applying pressure with his right hand on her back. They face each other on the "rock-step". On the "step", he holds his right hand out, and she responds by placing her left hand into it. They rotate their hands (man's left, woman's right) around to Standard Open Grip.

11. Switch to Open Position

"Slow, slow, quick, quick"

THE HISTORY OF JITTERBUG
PART ONE

Benny Goodman, the "King of Swing."

Cab Calloway.

Here's some background information about the Jitterbug:

- It began in the late twenties as the "Lindy Hop", named in honor of Charles Lindbergh. The inspiration: the Lindy consisted of a lot of "air steps" (feet off the floor), and Lindbergh was an aviator.

- For about ten years, the Lindy was done almost exclusively by blacks in big cities like New York and Chicago.

- It was the forerunner of today's dances — the first popular American dance ever based on improvised steps instead of a set pattern. Dancers could pretty much do whatever they felt like — all that counted was moving to the beat of the music.

- The name "Jitterbug" was reputedly coined by bandleader Cab Calloway in the early thirties. Calloway's orchestra played at hot spots like Harlem's Savoy Ballroom, where the Lindy Hoppers were as much a part of the show as the music. Calloway dubbed the frenzied dancers "Jitter Bugs".

- The first Jitterbug record was Calloway's 1934 tune, "Jitter Bug", a salute to the frantic Lindy Hoppers.

- Soon, Jitterbug became the popular term for the *dance* as well as the *dancers*.

- A Jitterbugger with fast feet was called a "flash dancer" at black dance clubs.

- Another Jitterbug innovation: dancing without touching your partner. Today it's common, but it originated with the Jitterbug. Black Lindy Hoppers created a move called the "breakaway", in which one of the dancers (usually the man) moved away from his partner and performed a series of acrobatic moves alone. Then the partners moved back together.

- The Jitterbug got really popular with white kids in 1936, when Benny Goodman brought his "swing" music to New York City's Paramount Theater. Teenage fans were so turned on by Goodman's music that they started jitterbugging in the aisles. It was so outrageous by thirties' standards that it made headlines all over the country.

- Swing music and Jitterbug swept across the country. For the first time, there was a music and style of dancing that belonged exclusively to the young. It set a precedent continued by rock'n'roll.

- As with rock'n'roll, adults thought the Jitterbug was undermining the nation's youth. It was banned in many dance halls. The Milwaukee Journal editorialized, for example: "If there is anything designed to . . .create consternation in the national bosom . . .it is undoubtedly the new dances. Proper persons have for years been viewing with alarm [this] shocking procession of new steps . . . ."

- As the thirties ended, the Jitterbug was a national craze. In 1938, over 25,000 people showed up in New York City for a "Carnival of Swing", featuring 26 bands and 7 hours of dancing (sounds like a rock festival). Jitterbug showed up in major films like the Marx Brothers' "A Day at the Races", specialty films like "Swing, Sister, Swing" and "The Prisoner of Swing", and even cartoons like "I'm Just a Jitterbug", featuring Mother Goose characters Jitterbugging their way through classic nursery rhymes. The 1939 World's Fair featured an electrifying exhibition of Jitterbugging couples. Kids hooked on Jitterbugging were called "Jive Addicts".

DR. JITTERBUG'S
PRESCRIPTIONS

DON'T SPREAD YOUR LEGS TOO FAR:
If you do, you're out of position for the next move. Then you have to overcompensate, and your whole rhythm is thrown off.

He's "stepping in the bucket" — moving his foot too far back

DON'T CRITICIZE YOUR DANCING PARTNER: It's impolite and unnecessary. No one likes to be told they dance poorly, even if it's true.

IF YOU'RE TALLER THAN YOUR PARTNER: Adjust your height to him or her. They can't get taller, so it's your responsibility. On a turn, for example, a tall man must be careful how high he raises his arm, a tall woman must make sure that man can get his arm over her head.

DON'T LOOK DOWN WHILE YOU DANCE: Beginners sometimes forget they're dancing WITH someone, and watch the floor instead of their partner. That looks terrible, and it's no fun.

DON'T STEP "IN THE BUCKET" WHEN YOU "ROCK" BACK: 6″ does it — any more, and you're throwing yourself off balance. Don't step so far back that you can't center your weight over your foot.

INTERMEDIATE

Congratulations! You've graduated from the Beginning Section. Now it's time for the moves that you've REALLY been waiting for — the ones that always impress people on a dance floor. The beauty of the Intermediate Moves is that they LOOK a lot more complicated than they are. You'll see that the footwork is pretty much the same for all of them . . . it's the hand movements that make them look sharp. And you'll see that these moves are directly built on the Beginning Moves.

Remember: take your time, relax, and have fun!

Go "All the Way" where?

INTERMEDIATE • MOVE 1
CEMENT MIXER

BUT I FELT LIKE A BIG DUMMY.

This step is very fast, so practice it to slow music, and try it a couple of times before you jump in and try it on the dance floor.

Make sure you allow your hands to turn — with a loose grip and palm-to-palm contact, and PLENTY of momentum. It begins with the first step after a "rock-step".

A

B

FIRST MOTION — Fig. A

MEN:
- Step 6″ to the left with left foot, pointing your toe to the left.

WOMEN:
- Step 6″ to right with right foot, pointing your toe to the right.

AS YOU STEP:
- Turn your body, facing direction of the step.
- Lift your arm (man's left, woman's right) as high as it'll go, making an arch over your head.

- Man's right, woman's left arm are extended down in opposite direction of arch. Maintain this relationship for the entire move.
- Keeping arms opposite each other is what makes the move look good.
- Transfer weight to ball of man's left, woman's right foot.
- COUNT: "Slow" (2 beats).

INTERMEDIATE • MOVE 1
CEMENT MIXER

I'm WILD about Jitterbug!

Me too!

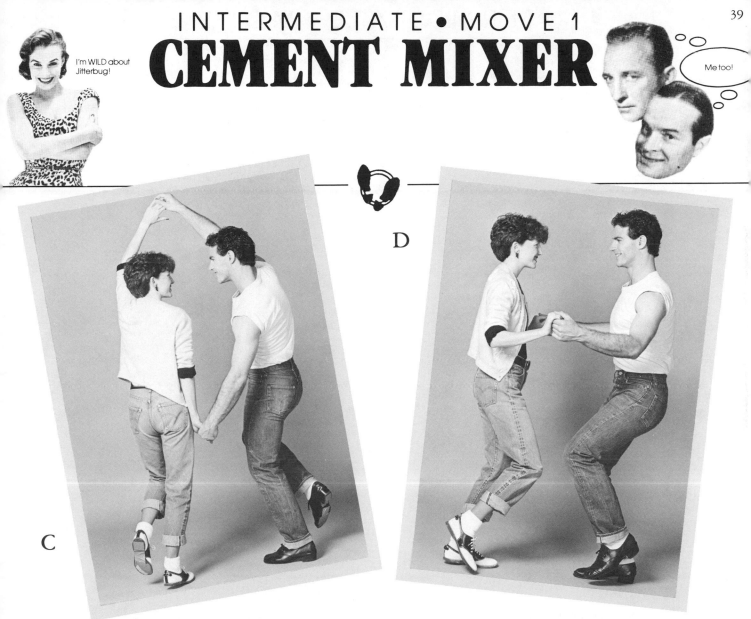

C

D

SECOND MOTION — Figs. B, C, D

MEN:
- Begin a step with right foot.

WOMEN:
- Begin a step with left foot.

AS YOU STEP:
- Raise your lower arm (man's right, woman's left) up and over your head, pivoting in place on one foot (man's left, woman's right).
- Go all the way around on one spin until you face each other.
- YOU GET THE MOMENTUM FOR YOUR SPIN FROM THE ARM MOVEMENT, SO BE FORCEFUL WITH IT.

WHEN FOOT LANDS:
- You are facing each other.
- Transfer weight to ball of man's right, woman's left foot.
- COUNT: "Slow" (2 beats).

NOW WITHOUT LOSING A BEAT, "ROCK-STEP" AND GO INTO A BASIC STEP

INTERMEDIATE • MOVE 2
SWEETHEART

This is a classic Jitterbug move that can be used with many variations (like the Yo-yo). The key is the "sweetheart position" (Fig. D). It begins out of the "rock-step" in a Basic.

The Jittermobile, 1947

I'll never forget the way we Jitterbugged last summer . . .

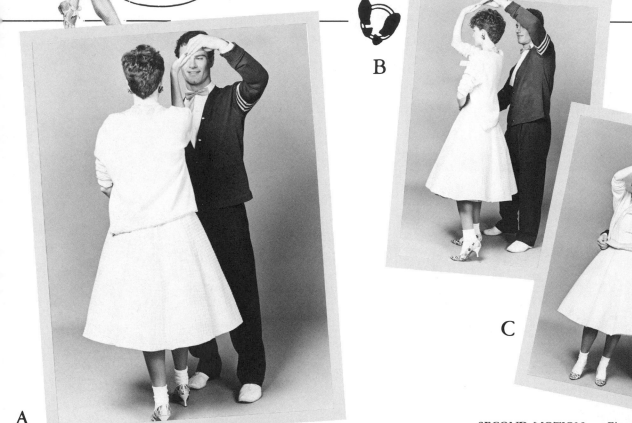

A

B

C

FIRST MOTION — Figs. A & B

MEN:

- Step in place with left foot, making a loop in front of you by raising left arm (forearm in front of forehead, hand by right ear). Begin turning partner counter-clockwise.

WOMEN:

- Step forward with right foot, beginning to turn to your left.
- Keep right elbow down.
- USE PALM-TO-PALM CONTACT.

AS FOOT LANDS:

- Transfer weight to ball of it.
- COUNT: "Slow" (2 beats).

SECOND MOTION — Fig. C

MEN:

- Step in place with right foot and loop left arm over partner's head like a lasso. Continue turning her until she is on your right, cradled into your right arm, facing the same direction as you.

WOMEN:

- Pivoting on your right foot, step back with left foot so you are side-by-side with man, facing the same direction.

WHEN FOOT LANDS:

- Transfer weight to ball of it.
- Woman is on man's right, cradled into his right arm (sweetheart position).
- Arms are relaxed, at waist level.
- COUNT: "Slow" (2 beats).

SWEETHEART

Life has never been better . . . and I owe it all to Jitterbug!

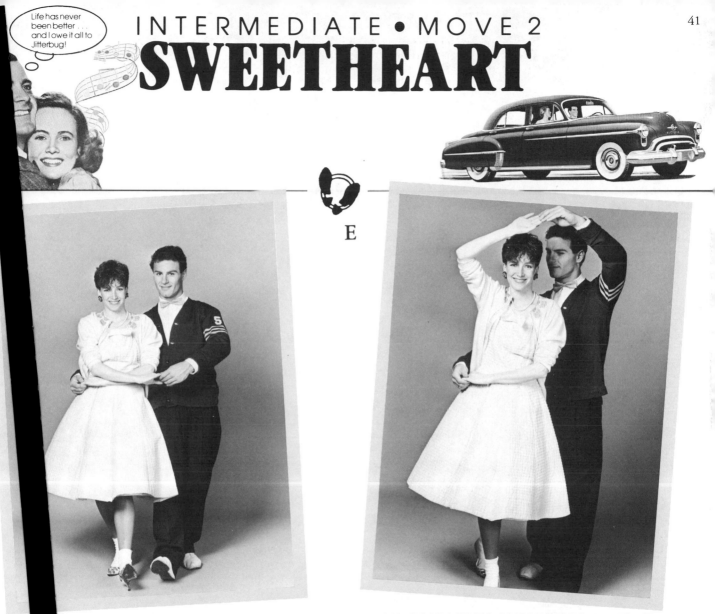

E

D

THIRD AND FOURTH MOTIONS:
The "Rock-step" — Fig. D

THIRD AND FOURTH MOTIONS:
The "Rock-step" — Fig. D

- "Rock" back together, bending slightly at the waist.
- "Step" together.

- COUNT: "Quick-quick" (2 beats).

TO GET BACK TO OPEN POSITION — Fig. E

MEN:
- Step in place with left foot, raising left arm above partner's head. Push gently on the small of her back with your right forearm, unrolling her under the arch. Step in place with right foot.

WOMEN:
- Step forward and across with right foot, under the arch. Then step around with left foot, pivoting right to face partner.
- COUNT: "Slow, slow" (4 beats).
- Then "rock-step", and you're back to a Basic.

The Rambler

This is a popular move. The arms are what you usually notice, but the feet are the key to making it look smooth. Take the time to get the footwork down pat. Then you can come out of the move and keep on dancing without losing a beat. A tip: practice the footwork alone, or without using your hands for awhile.

To start: Complete a Basic Step, but don't start another Basic. Your first step forward (after the "Rock-Step") will be the first step of the Shoulder Slide.

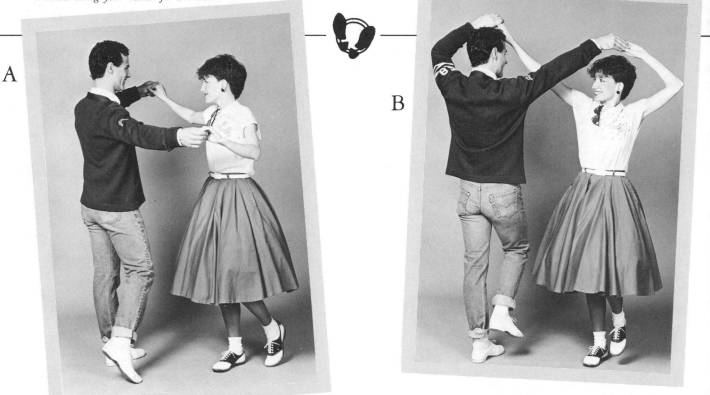

A

B

FIRST MOTION — Fig. A

MEN:
· Step forward and diagonally to the left about 8″ with left foot.

WOMEN:
· Step forward about 8″ with your right foot (slightly across your left foot if necessary).

AS YOU STEP:
· In one sweeping motion, push your arms down, out (away from body), then up (above shoulders).
· Twist to left, so your left shoulder goes back.

AS FOOT LANDS:
· Put all weight on the ball of it.
· Keep your rear heel off the floor.

COUNT:
· "Slow" (2 beats)

SECOND MOTION — Figs. B & C

MEN:
· Step forward with your right foot ACROSS your left foot (right is now a few inches in front of left).

WOMEN:
· Step forward about 8″ with your left foot.

AS YOU STEP:
· Bring your arms over and in back of your head (Fig. B) and rest your hands lightly on the back of your neck (Fig. C)
· Your arms are fully extended.
· You are side-to-side, facing opposite directions.

AS FOOT LANDS:
· Put all weight on the ball of it

COUNT:
· "Slow" (2 beats)

INTERMEDIATE • MOVE 3
SHOULDER SLIDE

JITTERBUG SEX

I wonder if he's a virgin

What a pompadour! Elvis sang some of the all-time greatest Jitterbug hits.

C

D

E

THIRD MOTION — Figs. D & E

MEN AND WOMEN:
· Release your partner's hand behind your head.
· Slide it down partner's arm (see Fig. D) simultaneously turning body ½-turn so you face each other.
AS YOU TURN:
· MEN: Step back on your left foot, pivoting on your right so both feet face partner.
· WOMEN: Step back on your right foot pivoting on your left so both feet face partner.
· Your right hands meet and catch each other (in shake-hands position).
· Your left hands are up in air
AS FOOT LANDS:
· Your rear foot is 6″ behind front foot, in "Rock" position.
· Weight is on ball of rear foot. Right arms are outstretched, dancers leaning slightly away from each other.
COUNT:
· "Quick" (1 beat)

The position you're in now is identical to Fig. B of the "Hand-Change" (Move 5). To complete the "Shoulder Slide", follow instructions for completing the "Hand-Change".

TEEN SCENE

JIVE TALK!

Pass the gravel, Gertie: "What's the news?"

Solid Jackson: A hep cat

Leather on Marble: A meat sandwich on white bread

Tumble, tumbleweed: "Scram!"

Moo with goo: Milk shake with ice cream

B'n'B: A tight couple, like Bogie and Bacall

Jeet?: Have you eaten yet?

Swoonderful: Dre-e-eamy

Croon another, Crosby: Tell me more

Let's Blast, here comes dynamite: Here comes a Slick Chick

Alive with Jive: Very hep

Morale Builder: A slick chick

Corner Casbah: Where the wolves hang out

Hi Humphrey, how's Bogart?: A greeting

Jive Junction: The "In" place to meet

Jet Propelled: Jitterbugger with super-fast feet

Strictly off the cob: In bad taste

Hubba, Boing, Ruff Ruff: Wolf calls

Atomic: Out of this world, Swoonderful

Give me a glass of water — here comes the pill: A real undesirable character is approaching

INTERMEDIATE BASIC

This is the same as the Beginning Basic Step, except that instead of ONE step for each of the "Slow" counts, you do TWO steps. This makes the Basic more fun. The Beginning Basic Step is good for fast songs, but you can use this Basic Step for most of the dances you do from now on. Refer to the Beginning Basic Step for details of this one.

A

B

FIRST MOTION — Figs. A & B

MEN:
Step 6″ to left with left foot (1 beat) as in Beginning Basic.
Bring right foot over & touch floor next to left foot with toes (right heel doesn't touch floor), leaning into step (1 beat).
Other details identical to Beginning Basic.
WOMEN:

· Step 6″ to right with right foot (1 beat) as in Beginning Basic
· Bring left foot over & touch floor next to right foot with toes (left heel doesn't touch floor), lean into step (1 beat).
· Other details identical to Beginning Basic.
WEIGHT REMAINS ON FOOT YOU FIRST STEPPED WITH.
· COUNT: "Slow" (2 beats).

C

SECOND MOTION — Fig. C

· Reverse the First Motion (opposite direction), man stepping to right, woman to left.

· COUNT: "Slow" (2 beats).
THE "ROCK-STEP" IS EXACTLY THE SAME AS IN THE BEGINNING BASIC.

"We had a swell time. Boy, he sure can Jitterbug!"

"M-m-m ...and what about AFTER the dance?"

Start in the closed position. Practice this at a slow tempo before you try it to music. The fun is in the timing of the kicks — doing them together — so concentrate on mastering that. Don't worry about the count while you do it — just get smooth.

A WORD OF CAUTION — watch out for other dancers and your partner when kicking.

THIS BEGINS AFTER THE "ROCK" OF THE "ROCK-STEP".

A

FIRST MOTION — The "Step"

MEN:
- Instead of stepping toward your partner on the "step" in the Closed Position, step across to the left with right foot.
- As you step, apply pressure on woman's back with your hand, steering her forward, side-to-side with you.

WOMEN:
- Partner's hand on your back, steering you forward as he moves with you is signal for Kicks.
- Instead of turning back toward your partner, step across to the right with left foot.

AT END OF "STEP":
- Couple is side-by-side.
- Weight is on ball of man's right, woman's left foot.

B

SECOND MOTION — Fig. A

- Still holding hands for Closed Position, man kicks out with left foot, woman kicks out with right foot.

WHEN FOOT LANDS:
- Transfer weight to ball of man's left, woman's right foot.
- COUNT: "Slow" (2 beats).

You'll feel better after a teaspoon of Dr. Jitterbug's Tonic!

Oooo . . . you sure know all the moves. Let's try that again!

C

D (optional)

THIRD MOTION — Fig. B

- Man kicks out with right foot, woman kicks with left foot.
- **AS YOU BRING YOUR FOOT DOWN:**
- Pivot on outside foot (man's left, woman's right), and completely reverse direction, so that by the time your foot touches the floor, it is pointing in the opposite direction.
- As you pivot, man bends left elbow, bringing his left and woman's right hand up to shoulder height.
- Continue holding both of partner's hands.
- **WHEN FOOT LANDS:**
- Transfer weight to ball of man's right, woman's left foot.
- Couple is side-by side.
- COUNT: "Slow" (2 beats).

FOURTH & FIFTH MOTIONS — Fig. C

- Couple kicks inside feet (Count: "slow" — 2 beats).
- Then you kick outside feet (Count: "slow" — 2 beats).
- **THEN:**
- Face each other, "rock-step", and return to basic.
- **OR:**
- Kick between legs facing each other, man's left and woman's right first (Fig. D).

THE HISTORY OF JITTERBUG
PART TWO

- The Jitterbug was still America's most popular dance in 1943, when trumpeter Harry James made a weeklong appearance at the Paramount Theater. He was greeted DAILY by lines of 8000 young Jitterbug fans who had to be controlled by mounted police.

- American GIs brought the dance to Europe during the war, and the Jitterbug quickly became as popular there as it was in the U.S.

- At the end of the war, America settled into a peaceful existence, and Jitterbugs became baby boom parents who no longer had any use for frenetic rhythms and rebellious fashions. Musical tastes became more sedate, and dance styles changed with them.

Harry James, who took America by storm with his trumpet.

- By the mid-fifties, American teenagers were fed up with pop music like the "Tennessee Waltz". They wanted something they could dance to.

- Bill Haley's "Rock Around the Clock" was the breakthrough. It hit the charts in 1955, bringing rock'n'roll dance music to whites. It was #1 for eight weeks.

- Kids modified the Jitterbug to go with Haley's music, making it a little slower and bouncier than it had been in the thirties. In some places it was still called the Jitterbug. In others, it was known as the Bop, or the Lindy, or the Rock'n'roll, the Swing etc. No matter — it was all basically the Jitterbug.

BE A JITTERBUG
CLOTHES MAKE THE JITTERBUG

Here are two Jitterbug costumes for gals.

'40s CHIC CHICK

Boy scout cap for that ultra-patriotic military look.

In the '40s, everyone took time for a little salute to our boys overseas.

Padded shoulders.

Tight-fitting suit is proper, but hard to dance in. Bring along jeans, just in case.

Never go out on a date without a pair of white gloves. Wear even when dancing.

Stockings are high class. Not showing: seams in back. If you haven't got stockings with seams, paint the seam-line on your leg like they did in the 40s.

High heels.

GREASER CHICK

Cool shades, indoors and out.

Carry a bunch of Jitterbug 45s around with you in case you run into a party.

Red Satin or Black Leather jacket.

Even greasers wear saddle shoes.

Chewing gum. Any kind, as long as you can crack it. Bubble gum for special occasions. Whenever someone starts to say something you don't want to hear, blow a bubble and pop it.

Oversized white shirt (steal one of your father's — it's good practice). Don't tuck it in; turn up the collar.

Faded blue jeans (don't even THINK about wearing designer jeans).

Roll up jeans to about 8" above ankles.

Bobby socks. If you don't have any, fold a pair of tube socks down so the stripes don't show.

INTERMEDIATE • MOVE 6
ST. CHARLES

Most of the action on this move is the man's. He loops his right and then his left arm over his head in rapid succession, and turns to face his partner. Apart from the fancy arm move, however, partners are basically just trading places, as in the Underarm Turn. This move starts after the "rock-step" of a Basic Step

A

B

C

FIRST MOTION — Fig. A

MEN:
· Make a loop in front of you with your right and your partner's left arm (arm across your chest, hand by left ear).
· Step forward and slightly to left with left foot, passing partner on YOUR right.
· Using palm-to-palm contact, put loop over your head, toward left shoulder (don't let go in midair).

WOMEN:
· Step forward and slightly to left with right foot, facing partner in quarter-turn.

AS FOOT LANDS:
· Transfer weight to ball of it.
· COUNT: "Quick" (1 beat).

SECOND MOTION — Figs. B & C

MEN:
· Drop 1st loop onto left shoulder and raise left hand, making a 2nd loop in front of you.
· Step forward, putting right foot in front of left and pointing toes slightly to left.
· As you step, bring left arm over your head, dropping left arm toward shoulder blade.

WOMEN:
· Pivoting to the right on ball of right foot, step back with left foot to face your partner's back.

AS FOOT LANDS:
· You are still holding both hands.
· Transfer weight to ball of it.
· COUNT: "Quick" (1 beat).

"I never knew you could dance so WELL, Gordon"

INTERMEDIATE • MOVE 6
ST. CHARLES

"Look dear — only 2 months old and she can already do the St. Charles!"

D

E

THIRD MOTION — Figs. D & E

MEN:
· Release woman's left hand with your right, & pivot around on right foot to face her as you step back with left foot into "rock" position.

WOMEN:
· As man turns to face you, step back into "rock" position with right foot.

AS YOU STEP:
· Man brings left arm down, rotating hand around woman's hand, and pushes off into "rock" position.
· COUNT: "Quick" (1 beat).

COUPLE COMPLETES THE "ROCK-STEP", AND CONTINUES INTO A BASIC STEP.

CROSSED-HANDS & ESCAPE

Look Good
...feel good
on your job

You have to know how to get in and out of the Crossed-Hands Position for many of the fancier moves in Jitterbug. To signal this position, the man holds out his free hand (usually his left) on the "step" after a Hand-Change. The woman must be watching his hands to see this signal, and the man must give it as early as possible, to allow her time to get her hand to his. If you're late in joining hands, your timing and smoothness are thrown off. Practice going into this position after a Reverse Underarm Turn, followed by a Hand-Change.

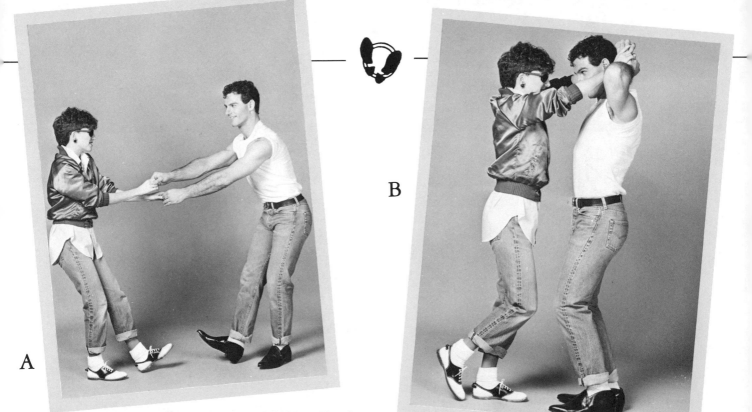

A

B

TO GET INTO CROSSED-HANDS POSITION — Fig. A

· Do a Reverse Underarm Turn, followed by a Hand-Change (see Figs. A & B, p. 24).
· "Rock-Step", holding right hands.
AS YOU "STEP":
· Man holds out his left hand, over his right. Woman takes it in her left hand.
· You are now in a Crossed-Hands Position.
· To get OUT of this position, use the "Standard Escape".

STANDARD ESCAPE, FIRST MOTION — Fig. B

AS THE COUPLE DOES A BASIC STEP IN PLACE:
· Bring both sets of hands over the man's head, resting on back of his neck. Man ducks, if necessary, to make this possible.

CROSSED-HANDS & ESCAPE

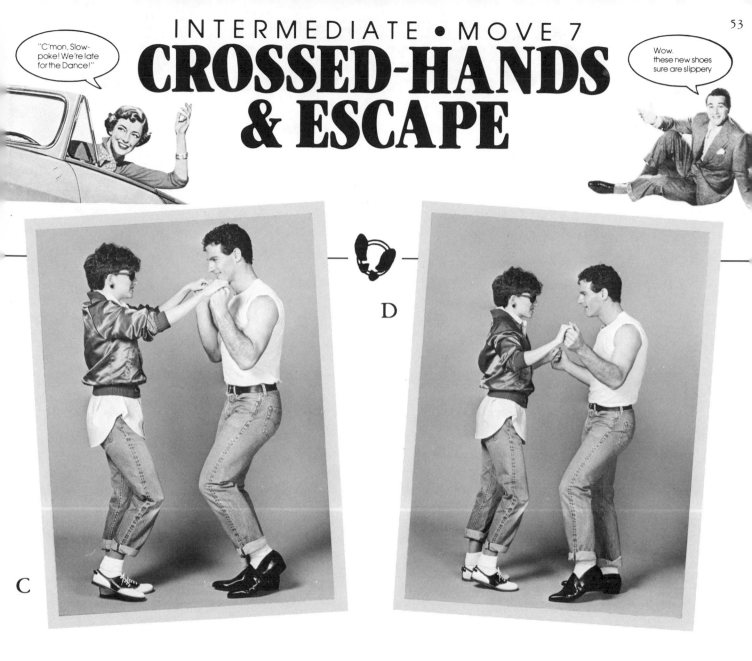

D

C

STANDARD ESCAPE, SECOND MOTION — Fig. C

· Without moving the arms, release the hands behind man's neck. Man's and woman's hands slide down and over the man's shoulders in mock-grip, man's left with woman's right, man's right with woman's left.

STANDARD ESCAPE, THIRD MOTION — Fig. D

· Hold hands out in Open Position, take proper grip, and return to Basic.

INTERMEDIATE • MOVE 8
CROSSED-HANDS TURN

This is essentially an Underarm Turn in Crossed-Hands Position, because you simply trade places in it.

TO START: Get in a Crossed-hands Position (see p. 52) as you

"rock-step". Your first step out of the "rock-step" will be the first step in this move.

TIP: Keep arms separated as in the Cement Mixer if you want to look really sharp.

A

B

FIRST MOTION — Figs. A & B

· Start in a crossed-hands position, left hands on top.

MEN:

· Raise your left hand, making an arch in front of partner as you step forward 6″ with left foot, passing her on YOUR right.

· Right hand is low, as in Cement Mixer.

WOMEN:

· Step forward 6″ with right foot, passing under the arch, turning away from partner as you step.

AS FOOT LANDS:

· Transfer weight to ball of it.

· COUNT: "Quick" (1 beat).

CROSSED-HANDS TURN

...and the kennel man told us how to avoid common dog ailments

D

"...are you cats and kittens ready for a little submarine race-watching?"

C

E

SECOND MOTION — Figs. C & D

MEN:
· Bring left hands down and simultaneously raise right hands over partner's head as you step with your right foot, pivoting to your left to face her.

WOMEN:
· Pivot counter-clockwise on the ball of your right foot as you step back with your left to face your partner.

AS FOOT LANDS:
· Transfer weight to ball of it.
· COUNT: "Quick" (1 beat). USE PALM-TO-PALM CONTACT AS YOU TURN

THIS MAY BE REPEATED ANY NUMBER OF TIMES, WITH THE WOMAN OR MAN TURNING, ONE PARTNER AT A TIME, IN EITHER DIRECTION — WHICHEVER THE HAND GRIP WILL ALLOW. YOU PASS ON OPPOSITE SIDES & TURN IN OPPOSITE DIRECTIONS EACH TIME.

TO RETURN TO OPEN POSITION:
· "Rock-step", using the Standard Escape to get back into Open Position as you do.

THE YO-YO

"I've never seen anyone move like that."

Jitterbug Romance

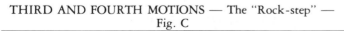

C

D

E

THIRD AND FOURTH MOTIONS — The "Rock-step" — Fig. C

- "Rock" back. Then as you "step", man gently pulls on woman's right arm, beginning to roll her in towards him. Woman begins to spin left, pivoting on the ball of her left foot.
- MAN RELEASES WOMAN'S LEFT HAND
- COUNT: "Quick-quick" (2 beats).

FIFTH AND SIXTH MOTIONS — The Spin — Figs. D & E

- Woman continues to spin all the way around until she faces partner. As she does, the man steps in place with left and right feet, with hands outstretched, waiting to catch woman's hands when she completes the spin.

AT THE END OF SPIN:
- Weight is on ball of man's right, woman's left foot, ready to "rock-step".
- Partners join hands in open position without missing a beat.
- COUNT: "Slow, slow" (4 beats).
- Complete the move with a "rock-step", and return to the Basic.

Dr. Jitterbug sez: Ladies, here are 3 never-fail excuses to avoid Nerds!

Dr. Jitterbug sez: Don't let this happen to you!

Oh no. I can't remember which side is my Left!

This begins with the couple in the SWEETHEART POSITION (p. 40), after the "rock-step" of the Sweetheart. There are 12 beats to it instead of the normal 6.

NOTE: *The woman must keep tension in her arms, or she won't feel the turn lead. And if the man pulls too hard, the woman will go flying*

A

FIRST MOTION — Fig. A

SECOND MOTION — Fig. B

FROM THE SWEETHEART POSITION:

MEN:
· Step in place with your left foot. As you step, release partner's right hand with your left and pull gently with your right hand, rolling her out to your side.

WOMEN:
· Step to the right with your right foot, beginning to spin to the right.

AS FOOT LANDS:
· Transfer weight to the ball of man's left, woman's right foot.
· COUNT: "Slow" (2 beats).

MEN:
· Step in place with right foot, continuing to roll partner out to right side. Keep your arm straight out to your side.

WOMEN:
· Continue spinning to your right, now on ball of right foot, until you face your partner. Then put left foot down.

WHEN FOOT LANDS:
· Man's left and woman's right arms are extended, with woman facing man's side.
· Weight is on ball of man's right and woman's left foot, ready to "rock-step".
· COUNT: "Slow" (2 beats).

For most minor ailments, I recommend Dr. Jitterbug's Extra-Strength Motion Potion

SHE GOES, HE GOES

This move is an option for the man in the Reverse Underarm Turn. Throw it in now and then to give the move a little flair. It looks sharp.

It involves an extra movement in the Reverse Underarm Turn, but no extra beats. It all takes place on the second ("slow") count of the move. To start: do a Basic, an Underarm Turn, and begin a Reverse Underarm Turn.

"I'll be ready in a minute . . ."

A

B

C

This move begins after Fig. B in the Reverse Underarm Turn (p. 22). Weight is on the man's left and woman's right foot. They've each stepped forward.

After the woman has gone under the "window", the man brings her hand down slightly to indicate the end of her turn. Normally, your hands would continue down as you turned to face each other (Fig. C, p. 23). But on this move, the man raises the hands again, making an arch high enough for him to go under, too.

Still facing forward, he steps forward with his right foot, under the arch and quickly pivots to his left on his left foot so that by the time his right foot lands, he is facing his partner.

The couple then rocks back into a "rock-step".

DR. JITTERBUG'S
PRESCRIPTIONS

Watch out for this guy!

WHAT HAPPENS IF YOU MESS UP A MOVE IN THE MIDDLE OF A DANCE?

Even the best dancers do it. Try to make it look as good as possible, keeping the beat and moving as smoothly as you can. In other words, FAKE IT. Actually, some of the best-known Jitterbug moves were invented by people who were covering up mistakes. You might invent some too.

DO YOU WIND UP FREQUENTLY BANGING INTO OTHER DANCERS ON THE FLOOR . . . INCLUDING YOUR PARTNER?

A good dancer remembers these rules:

- The Jitterbug needs lots of space, so sometimes it's hard to keep from bumping into people on a crowded dance floor. If that's the case, remember: the man is responsible for his partner's safety. Don't lead her into a turn when you know she's going to collide with someone.
- There's always a couple that thinks they've got a right to dance wherever they want — even if it's on YOUR foot. Don't be one of these jerks. Respect other dancers' space.
- Be aware of where your partner is at all times, to avoid accidents. You can really hurt your partner if you're careless, and no one wants to dance with a Kamikaze pilot.

You can really injure your partner with carelessness!

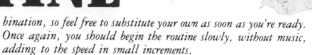

INTERMEDIATE ROUTINE

I've never had so much fun.

The Intermediate Routine includes most of the moves in the Intermediate Section and some from the Beginning Section. The idea is to give you an understanding of how you can use moves in combination, so feel free to substitute your own as soon as you're ready. Once again, you should begin the routine slowly, without music, adding to the speed in small increments.

1. Intermediate Basic Step in Open Position

"Slow, slow, quick, quick"

2. Intermediate Basic Step in Open Position

"Slow, slow, quick, quick"

TRANSITION: On "step" of "rock-step", man begins to raise his right arm (woman's left), making a window by bringing his forearm across his forehead, hand to right ear. Woman begins turning counter-clockwise.

3. Sweetheart

"Slow, slow, quick, quick"
"Slow, slow, quick, quick"

TRANSITION: On "step" of "rock-step", man begins raising his right arm (woman's left) to put it over his head, couple assumes passing position (right side to right side).

4. St. Charles

"Quick, quick, quick, quick"

TRANSITION: As couple completes move, they face each other holding one hand (man's left to woman's right). Man moves into passing position (left side to left side) as they "rock-step". On "step" of "rock-step", man begins to raise his left (woman's right) arm, making an arch in front of the woman.

5. Underarm Turn

"Quick, quick, quick, quick"

TRANSITION: On "step" of "rock-step", man raises left arm, making a window. Couple looks at each other through the window.

6. Reverse Underarm Turn, with a Hand-Change

"Quick, quick, quick, quick"

TRANSITION: At end of second count, as couple begins the "rock-step", man transfers woman's right hand into his right hand. As they "step" on the "rock-step", man holds out his left hand over their right hands, and woman places her left hand into it.

7. Crossed-Hands Position

TRANSITION: Couple goes directly into the Crossed-Hands Turn, with first step after the "rock-step" being the first step of the turn.

8. Crossed-Hands Turn
"Slow, slow, quick, quick"

TRANSITION: As couple does the "step" in the "rock-step", they begin raising their hands (in Crossed-Hands position) toward the man's head. If man will have to duck to get the hands over his head, he begins on the "step".

9. Standard Escape
"Slow, slow, quick, quick"

TRANSITION: Couple is in Open Position, facing each other.

10. Intermediate Basic Step in Open Position
"Slow, slow, quick, quick"

TRANSITION: On first step after "rock-step", man steps to the left, pointing toes left, and woman steps to the right, pointing toes right. They are shoulder-to-shoulder, with arms in an arch over their heads on first count.

11. Cement Mixer
"Slow, slow, quick, quick"

TRANSITION: On "step" of "rock-step", couple assumes passing position (right side to right side) and begins moving forward, sweeping arms up and out.

12. Shoulder Slide
"Slow, slow, quick, quick"

TRANSITION: At end of Shoulder Slide, couple is facing each other in a Hand-Change position. On the "step" of the "rock-step", they begin passing each other (right side to right side) as man makes an arch in front of woman with his right (her right) arm.

13. Behind-the-Back Hand-Change
"Slow, slow, quick, quick"

TRANSITION: Couple faces each other, holding one hand (man's left, woman's right). On "step" of "rock-step", man raises his left (woman's right) arm, forearm across his forehead and hand at right ear, making a window as if they're doing the Reverse Underarm Turn. Woman begins turning counter-clockwise.

14. Inside Underarm Turn with She Goes, He Goes
"Slow, slow, quick, quick"

TRANSITION: Couple faces each other holding one hand (man's left, woman's right). As they step, he holds out his right hands and woman places her left in it.

15. Intermediate Basic Step in Open Position
"Slow, slow, quick, quick"

BE A JITTERBUG
TEST YOUR JITTERBUG I.Q.

Answers are on page 63.

What's on his mind?
See question #5

1) What hair product cautioned that "a little dab'll do ya"?
2) What Hep Cat was known as the "Hi-de-Ho-Man"?
3) What is a "licorice stick" in Swing?
4) Was there really someone named Runaround Sue? What was Dion's relationship to her?
5) Why would a girl wear a ring around her neck? Who did a song about it?
6) Name the Jitterbug toothpaste:
   a) It had Gardol's "invisible shield"
   b) Bucky Beaver defeated Mr. Tooth Decay every time
   c) You wondered "where the yellow went"
7) Who recorded *Queen of the Hop*?
8) Who is "dreamier" — Fabian or Pat Boone?
9) What are falsies?
10) Will he still respect me in the morning?
11) What do you call a waitress in a drive-in restaurant?
12) Which DJ is credited with inventing the term "Rock and Roll"?
13) Match the group with its leader
    a) Frankie Lymon and the . . .   a) Thundering Herd
    b) Woody Herman and his . . .   b) Tennessee Three
    c) Carl Perkins and the . . .   c) Teenagers
14) Which Everly Brothers' tune is better to Jitterbug to?
    a) *All I have To Do is Dream*
    b) *Wake Up Little Susie*
15) What does "D.A." stand for in a D.A. hair cut?
16) If a girl is "pinned", does that mean she's a wrestler?
17) What are Pez?
18) What instrument did Les Paul play? Who was his partner?

Why is this couple smiling?
See question #16.

Why is she smiling?
See question #9

19) According to Frankie Avalon, what happens when "a girl changes from Bobby Socks to Stockings"?

20) Let's say a greaser arrives at the drive-in with his Indian. What does the Indian look like?

21) Who was the "Wild One"?

22) Which 1957 car is probably the Jittermobile of all time?

23) Name the Bopper who recorded each of these tunes:
   a) Boppin' the Blues
   b) Be-Bop-A-Lula
   c) Be-Bop Baby

24) What do you wear to a prom, according to Marty Robbins?

25) Which famous band leader was killed during World War II?

26) Where was the original McDonald's drive-in restaurant (in the late '40s)?

27) Why would a Jitterbug wear a bee-hive?

28) Who was James Dean's co-star in "Rebel Without A Cause" (female lead)?

29) Which Philadelphia TV celebrity suggested that Danny and the Juniors change the title of their new song from *Do the Bop* to *At the Hop* ?

30) What happens if you put an aspirin in a Coke?

"Me Complain? Never!"

ANSWERS

14) b — *Wake Up Little Susie, All I Have To Do Is Dream* is one of the classic slow songs.
    c-b
    b-a
13) a-c
12) Alan Freed.
11) A car-hop.
10) Probably not.
9) You don't know?
8) Neither.
7) Bobby Darin, who also did the Jitterbug classic, *Splish Splash.*
   c) Pepsodent.
   b) Ipana.
6) a) Colgate Dental Cream.
5) She'd wear it on a chain because she was going steady. Elvis did *Wear My Ring* in 1958.
4) Yes. In real life, he married her.
3) A clarinet.
2) Cab Calloway.
1) Brylcreem.

30) Ask someone who tried it on his date.
29) Dick Clark.
28) Natalie Wood.
27) It's a woman's hair-do.
26) San Bernadino, California.
25) Glenn Miller.
24) A white sport coat and a pink carnation.
   c) Ricky Nelson.
   b) Gene Vincent or the Everly Brothers.
23) a) Carl Perkins
22) A '57 Chevy, of course.
21) Marlon Brando, in the 1954 flick of the same name.
20) It's a motorcycle. Indian is a classic make that's a prized collector's item.
19) "She's old enough to give her heart away."
18) Guitar, Mary Ford.
17) Little brick-like candies that came in keen dispensers with cartoon heads on them.
16) No. It means she's engaged to be engaged.
15) Duck's Ass.

Before Jitterbug

After Jitterbug

CREATE YOUR OWN MOVES
JITTERBUG VARIATIONS

Every move you learn in this book can be adapted to create other moves. Sometimes, in fact, a little flair is all you need to make a move look entirely different on the dance floor. Experiment — try out your ideas. Add excitement to your dance routines. Here are a few examples of ways you can vary moves you've already learned. After you've checked them out, start coming up with YOUR OWN!

- **ON A 1-HAND LEAD:** As you do the Basic Step, try moving in toward your partner so you're right in front of each other. Then move away as you "rock-step". The action is like an accordion — IN on the "Slow-Slow", OUT on the "quick-quick".

- **ON A 1-HAND LEAD:** Try doing the Basic with man's left, woman's right arm extended the whole time. Travel in a circle as you dance. You can throw your other hand up in the air while you do the step, like the photo on the cover of this book.

- **IN CLOSED POSITION:** Try "Cheek-to-Cheek". Do the whole Basic Step with man's right and woman's left cheek touching, facing man's left and woman's right the entire time.

- **VARY THE UNDERARM TURN:** Instead of the man raising his left arm to HIS LEFT for the Underarm Turn, raise it to the right; the woman then passes him on his right side. This is called the "Inside Underarm Turn", and it's essentially the same as the Reverse Underarm Turn — only it's done after the Basic Step instead of following an Underarm Turn.

- **AFTER A BASIC IN THE OPEN POSITION:** Either the woman, or both partners, take a free spin. That means letting both hands go, spinning all the way around until partners face each other again, and taking each other's hands in Open Position again, without losing a beat. To start: as you begin the first step of a Basic, man lets go of woman's right hand with his left, and begins to spin her with his right hand, releasing the hand as she spins. To follow this lead, woman must have tension in her arms.

- **IN SWEETHEART POSITION:** After you "rock", don't "step" — keep walking backwards, circling with the man's left foot as the pivot point. Escape with the Yo-Yo move.

- **CROSSED-HANDS ESCAPE:** Instead of the Standard Crossed-Hands Escape, do an Underarm Turn in Crossed-Hands Position, letting go of ONE hand as the woman goes under the arch. You are then facing each other in a Hand-Change Position, and should know what to do next.

- **THERE'S A FEW — NOW YOU TRY.**

ADVANCED

Now we get to the really fancy stuff — the moves that the "pros" do. Some of the Advanced Moves are built on previous moves in the book — the Texas Tommy, for example. But others are completely new. These are the acrobatic moves called "Lifts".

Lifts are classic Jitterbug moves. They are spectacular to watch, and everyone wants to do them. But the truth is that not everyone SHOULD do them. They are very physically demanding, requiring strength and coordination. And there's a risk that you and your partner could get hurt doing them. Only YOU can decide if you're capable of doing them safely — their inclusion here is not an open endorsement for you to try them. But if you do decide to try them, then remember — **SAFETY FIRST!** And read page 68 carefully before you start.

DR. JITTERBUG'S
PRESCRIPTIONS

The wrong way to lead your partner

Hold on to your partner

SAVE THE WRESTLING FOR AFTER THE DANCE: With a physical dance like Jitterbug, it's easy for the man to accidentally be too forceful in his leads. So take care, guys, not to squeeze your partner's hand too tightly; don't push, pull, yank, haul, tackle, or trip your partner; and if you have to bend her arm, do it GENTLY!

REMEMBER: SAFETY COMES FIRST WHEN YOU'RE DOING "LIFTS".
Be absolutely sure you can handle the acrobatic moves before you try them! On the other moves, the worst that can happen if you make a mistake is stepping on your partner's toe. But on a lift you can really hurt yourself or your partner.

- Loosen up before you try a lift.
- Talk it through with your partner before you try it — be sure you both know what to expect. You can do a dry run on other types of moves, but once you start a lift, you're committed.
- Check out ceiling heights before you start.
- Make sure you're physically capable of what's required in a lift. Don't do the Shoot-Thru, for example, if you have a bad back.
- Don't try them in a crowd.
- Make sure you've got a good grip on your partner, and wipe off sweaty hands before you start.
- If the man is not strong enough to lift his partner, admit it!

The heartbreak of not knowing how to Jitterbug.

TEEN SCENE

Jitterbug Sex:

Oh no, he really DOES have etchings!

67

Are you in the know?

When giving a party, which is important?

☐ Fancy refreshments ☐ Banishing the family ☐ Keeping the guests busy

If your back's blemished, what's best?

☐ A white hanky
☐ A rain check
☐ A stole

What's the jinx in this jalopy?

☐ The cuddle couple
☐ The boogie blast
☐ Four's a crowd

When you don't know the party guests, should you

☐ Plunge in boldly ☐ Pause at the doorway

Which lipstick makes teeth look whiter?

☐ Blue-red ☐ Orange-red ☐ Brown-red

Are you in the know?

How to straighten out a feud you started?

☐ Make the first move
☐ Wait for him to call
☐ Try the weeping technique

They all Laughed
when I said
I could Cook!

**They didn't know
I had practiced on my family**

Jitterbug? Dahling, I thought you'd never ask!

FAINTING

Jitterbug Sex: If he says "Yes," will I still respect him in the morning?

This move is easy to recognize on the dance floor, because the first two motions are unique to it. Woman keeps tension in her arms so man can lead the spin, but makes her spin more of a PIVOT so she can stop halfway around, with her back to him. The man should accommodate this by guiding her into the spin rather than spinning her hard. Practice it slowly so you get the timing right, and the movement smooth. Man must keep his arms rigid when he catches her falling back. Begin the move after the "rock-step" of a Basic.

A

B

FIRST MOTION — Fig. A

MEN:
- As you step with left foot to begin basic, extend your left arm and pull right hand in toward you. This twists your partner's upper body to her right.

WOMEN:
- As you step right to begin Basic, allow partner to swivel you to your right, but put extra tension in your arms.
- COUNT: "Slow" (2 beats).

SECOND MOTION — Fig. B

MEN:
- As you step right on 2nd motion of Basic, swivel partner to her left, extending your right arm and pulling in your left.

WOMEN:
- Partner swivelling you to left is signal he's going to spin you. Put tension in left arm, preparing for next motion, as you step left in 2nd Motion of Basic.
- COUNT: "Slow" (2 beats).

ADVANCED • MOVE 1
FAINTING

C

D

E

THIRD MOTION — Fig. C

MEN:
- Step in place with left foot as you spin woman clockwise, releasing her right hand with your left and spinning her with your right hand. When she begins to spin, release other hand too. Hold arms straight in front of you.

WOMEN:
- Spin to your right, pivoting on left foot, until your back is to man. Extend both arms out to your side, making a "T".
- COUNT: "Slow" (2 beats).

FOURTH MOTION — Figs. D & E

MEN:
- As woman falls back toward you, stiffen arms and catch her under her arms, bending knees to accommodate her backward motion.
- When she's fallen back as far as you'll let her, smoothly re-bound, raising her as you straighten your knees.
- When she's standing, gently push her right arm with your right hand, spinning her clockwise to face you.

WOMEN:
- Point your left foot out as you "faint" back into man's arms, bending right knee.
- Straighten knee as man lifts you to standing position.
- Pivot on right foot as man spins you to face him.
TAKE EACH OTHER'S HANDS IN OPEN POSITION, AND RETURN TO BASIC.

ADVANCED • MOVE 2
TEXAS TOMMY

I Know My Necking

This move is easiest when started from a One-hand Lead. Practice it slowly to get the footwork down (after you understand the hand movement, of course). The hardest part for both partners is to come out of the spin into a "rock-step", so work on it. The hand-change is not shown at the end, but is part of the move. Getting the woman's spin to be smooth also takes some work for beginners. Your first step out of a "rock-step" will be the first step of this move.

A

B

IN "STEP" OF "ROCK-STEP" OUT OF ONE-HAND LEAD, MAN PULLS WOMAN FORWARD, AS

CLOSE TO HIM AS POSSIBLE, SETTING UP THIS MOVE

FIRST MOTION — Figs. A & B

MEN:

· Step past your partner with left foot, gently pushing her right arm behind her back. Lean forward and reach around her waist on the other side with yor right hand.

WOMEN:

· Step forward and slightly across with right foot. When you feel man pushing your arm back, BEND IT UP TO THE SMALL OF YOUR BACK.

AS FOOT LANDS:

· Man places woman's right hand into his right hand (behind her back).
· Woman bends left arm up toward body (or points it straight up).
· Transfer weight to ball of man's left, woman's right foot.
· COUNT: "Slow" (2 beats).

ADVANCED • MOVE 2
TEXAS TOMMY

"Howdy, partner."

C

D

E

THIRD MOTION — Fig. E

MEN:
Pivot on right foot to face your partner, stepping back with left into "rock" position. Switch her hand into your left hand as you begin "rock". Place it — don't throw it!

WOMEN:
· Continue your spin, now on your left foot, until you face your partner, with right foot landing back in "rock" position.

AS FOOT LANDS:
· Transfer weight to ball of it.
· Arms are extended.
· Couple faces each other.

· COUNT: "Quick" (1 beat).

Complete the "rock-step" and go back into a Basic.

WORDS OF CAUTION:
· When man leans over in First Motion, don't bang heads.
· If move is uncomfortable for woman, either man's hand is too high on the hand-change, or too high on the unrolling.
. If the woman's hand is bent back too high on First Motion, it's a wrestling hold, not dancing.
· Use palm-to-palm contact on hand-change to avoid injury.

SECOND MOTION — Figs. C & D

MEN:
· Step past and around your partner with right foot, beginning to turn right to face her as you pull gently on her right arm, unrolling her like a yo-yo.

WOMEN:
· Spin clockwise on your right foot, lowering your left to the floor when your back is to your partner.

AS FOOT LANDS:
· Transfer weight to ball of it.
· COUNT: "Slow" (2 beats).

ADVANCED • MOVE 3
FALLBACKS

"Here's Jitter-bugging with YOU, kid."

I warn you, the Jitterbug is a Communist plot!

The easiest of the "acrobatic" moves, and one of the most fun. Be sure you've got a good grip on your partner before you let go — wipe off sweaty hands before trying it. And when your hand goes back, *remember that arc. That gives the move class. Don't worry about the rhythm at first — just make the move smooth.*

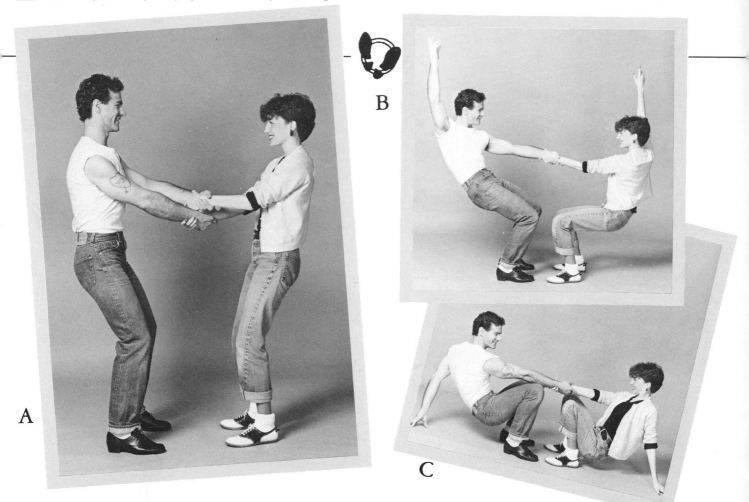

A

B

C

STARTING POSITION — Fig. A

· Man and woman face each other in a crossed-hands position, but with one variation: you are wrist-to-wrist. Instead of holding each other's hands, you hold your partner's wrists. This is necessary, because it prevents your grip from slipping when you're leaning back.
· If it takes a while to get into this grip, do a Basic while you get set.

FIRST MOTION — Figs. B & C

· Release your top hands and swing your arms smoothly overhead in an arc.
· Bend your knees and lean away from each other, using partner's weight to support you.
· Continue bending knees as you swing your arm in back of you.
· Touch your hand on the floor without sitting down.

Don't step on this guy's Blue Suede Shoes!

ADVANCED • MOVE 3
FALLBACKS

CENSORED

Dr. Jitterbug sez: Don't let this happen to you — Learn to Jitterbug today!

E

D

SECOND MOTION — Fig. D

· Stand up forcefully, helping each other up by pulling on partner's wrist, swinging arm over your head in an arc.
· Connect wrist-to-wrist again.

THIRD & FOURTH MOTION — Fig. E

· Now repeat the motion using opposite hands, swinging arms smoothly overhead as you bend your knees and fall back away from each other, hands touching the floor.

Push off the floor and come back to standing position. TO RETURN TO OPEN POSITION, USE STANDARD ESCAPE (P. 52)

ADVANCED • MOVE 4
LEGOVER

Jitterbug is great exercise

This is a sharp move when done SMOOTHLY. It can also be a dangerous one. If the woman bends over too far, she could get kicked in the head. So practice it to find out the safe distance for the woman — and the height at which the arms should be held to allow the man to step over comfortably. For smoothness, the man should work on his spin. REMEMBER: SAFETY FIRST!

A

B

AS YOU DO A "ROCK-STEP" — Fig. A

- Man lets go of woman's right hand with his left as they "rock".
- Man pushes down with a stiff, straight arm as they "step". This is the signal for the Leg-Over; woman stays back to avoid man's foot, bending to the left by lowering her left shoulder and bending her knees.

FIRST MOTION — Figs. A, B & C

MEN:
- Lift left leg and swing it over your right arm, woman's left.
- As soon as it clears, let go of her hand and pivot on your right foot until your back is to your partner.

WOMEN:
- Adjust your height to make sure man clears the arms. As soon as his leg clears, let go. Step in place with right foot.
- COUNT: "Slow" (2 beats).

Jitterbug's a GAS

ADVANCED • MOVE 4
LEGOVER

C

D

SECOND MOTION — Fig. D

MEN:
- Continue your turn, spinning on left foot this time, until you face your partner.
- Catch her left hand with your right.

WOMEN:
- Step in place with left foot as he spins. Hold out your left hand for him to catch.

WHEN FOOT LANDS:
- Weight is on man's right, woman's left foot.
- DO A "ROCK-STEP". HOLDING MAN'S RIGHT, WOMAN'S LEFT HAND. THEN RETURN TO OPEN POSITION AND BASIC STEP.

THE HISTORY OF JITTERBUG
PART THREE

- 1956 was the year that rock'n'roll took hold the way swing had twenty years before. It was the year of Elvis, Little Richard, Fats Domino, Jerry Lee Lewis, Chuck Berry. History repeated itself: adults claimed rock'n'roll was ruining America's youth, and banned the music and/or the dancing in public places all over America.

- Of course, the craze continued. Rock'n'roll dancing gradually became acceptable.

- The strongest influence on popular dancing in the late fifties was American Bandstand. It began as a local Philadelphia dance program, and in 1957, ABC TV decided to broadcast it nationally. Soon, Dick Clark was host to 20 million people every weekday, as America tuned in to watch the Bandstand regulars show off the latest dance moves.

Dick Clark's American Bandstand did more to spread rock'n'roll dancing than any other single influence.

- With the advent of the Twist in 1960, dance styles changed. People didn't touch each other when they danced anymore, and the Jitterbug faded in popularity.

- In the seventies, a wave of nostalgia swept America. *American Grafitti* and *Happy Days* made the fifties popular again. There were rock'n'roll "revivals", which included Jitterbugging. Since then, the dance has steadily made a place for itself again.

Maybe NOW he'll notice me . . .

BE A JITTERBUG
CLOTHES MAKE THE JITTERBUG

Here are two more Jitterbug outfits for your next sock hop.

I Stepped into a Big-Pay Hotel Job

BOBBY SOXER

Smile sweetly. And remember: lipstick makes you look like a Grown-Up.

You love to listen to those dreamy songs about true love.

A Circle Skirt. Of course, a Poodle Skirt is the utmost. But any Circle Skirt is great for dancing. When you spin, it flies out and you look unbelievably cool.

Lots of petticoats underneath. When you spin, everyone's gonna see 'em, so wear bright colors. Red is great.

Saddle shoes for all occasions.

Cat's-Eye Sunglasses. Bright-colored plastic. Chew on the stems instead of gum.

A necklace made of pop-beads is ultra-swoonderful.

Monogrammed shirt. Or, if you're really with-it, have your whole name spelled out. Tip: If you want to make your own, use beads or sequins. This one is spelled out completely with beads.

Surprise! Bobby-soxers don't ONLY wear bobby socks. Anklets are OK too.

MR. NICE GUY

Clean-shaven face. And always be polite. Eddie Haskell is your hero.

Remember this little rhyme: "Nice guys wear Bow Ties". Your date's parents will love it.

Letter sweater. Preferably your own, but what the hell — it's the impression that counts. Any cardigan will do in a pinch.

A little "hair oil" keeps hair in place. Caution: Don't use so much that your date will need a towel when she runs her fingers through it.

White shirt.

Frankie Lymon and the Teenagers album reveals secret love of rock 'n' roll and Jitterbugging.

Baggy, pleated pants (Jeans for Saturday only). Always pressed, with nice crease.

Loafers or white bucks are standard footwear. If you haven't got either, paint an old pair of shoes white.

THE TUNNEL

NO DOUBT ABOUT IT!

This is a fancy move that looks harder than it is. It always gets attention. The man essentially stands in one place, concentrating on arm movement. The woman does most of the body movement, walking around in back of her partner, and then backing around, re-tracing her steps until she's in starting position again. The key is switching hand-grips to make her travelling possible. Practice slowly, paying little attention to the music until you're ready to back into a Basic.

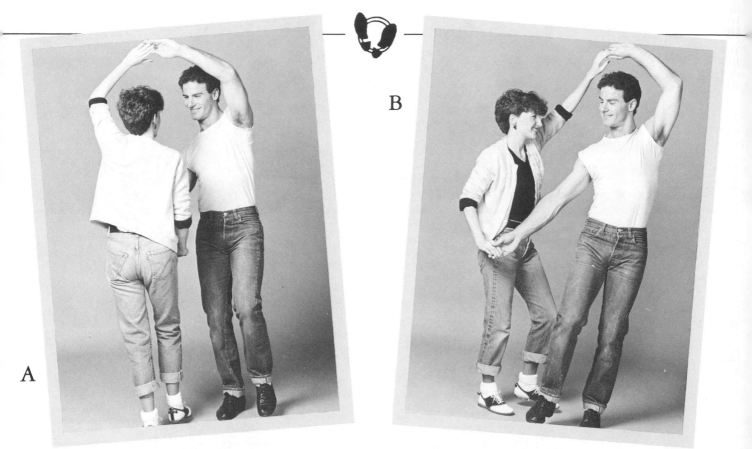

A

B

FIRST MOTION — Fig. A

- Man and woman face each other in Crossed-Hands Position, left hands on top.
MEN:
- Step forward 6″ with left foot, passing woman on YOUR right.
- Make an arch with your left (woman's left) arm, raise it over your head.
- Keep right hand (woman's right) down LOW. This is VERY IMPORTANT!
WOMEN:
- Step 6″ with right foot, passing man on YOUR right
- Keep right hand low. VERY IMPORTANT.

SECOND MOTION — Fig. B

AT THIS POINT, FORGET THE FOOTWORK AND JUST TRAVEL THROUGH THE ARM MOTIONS.
MEN:
- Put the arch over your own head, bringing left arm in back of head.
- Extend right arm, with loose grip.
WOMEN:
- Begin to travel around man's back, facing him.

ADVANCED • MOVE 5
THE TUNNEL

The Statesman

C

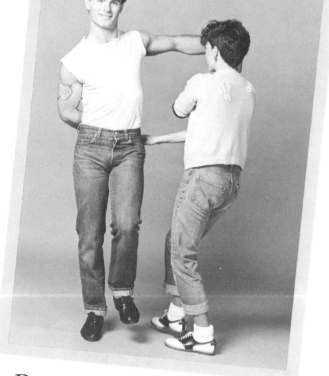

D

THIRD MOTION — Fig. C

MEN:
- Bring right hand up to small of back, gripping loosely so partner's hand can turn in yours.
- Extend left arm (not necessarily as fully as shown), keeping hand open so partner can rotate hand around yours. Do not grip her hand.

WOMEN:
- Travel to man's left, facing him.
- Rotate your left hand around in his (flip it over) so yours is on top, fingertips in his palm. THIS IS ESSENTIAL!
- Continue holding his hand behind his back.

FOURTH MOTION — Fig. D

MEN:
- Bring left hand back as you raise your left elbow in back of you, making a window.
- Make it as big as possible, as woman is going under it.
- Keep loose grip; palm-to-palm contact.

WOMEN:
- Pivot clockwise to face man's left arm (window). DUCK, bending knees and dropping head slightly — this depends on your size, relative to your partner.

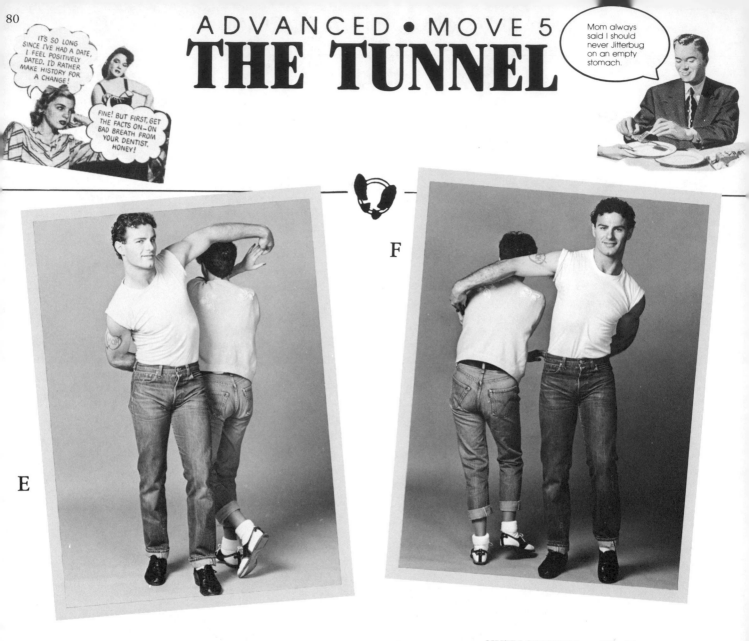

E

F

FIFTH MOTION — Fig. E

MEN:
· As woman travels under your arm, raise it even further until you're sure she can get through.
· Continue holding her right hand, behind your back.

WOMEN:
· Walk under man's left arm. Duck as much as you have to.

SIXTH MOTION — Fig. F

MEN:
· When partner has gone under your arm, lower left arm and step to the left with left foot, keeping your back to partner.
· Lean slightly left and begin to raise right elbow.

WOMEN:
· Back up to your left as you pivot clockwise.
· As you move, you're back-to-back with partner.
· Back up until you get to his left arm.

EIGHTH MOTION — Fig. H

MEN:
· Release her left hand with your left hand as she backs away from you.
· Both her hands are in your right hand.
· As she drops her right hand from yours, you grip her left with your right.
· Hold out left hand, get in Open position, begin a Basic.

WOMEN:
· As you back out, stand.
· Both your hands are in his right hand.
· Drop your right hand, take partner's left hand with it.
· You are in Open Position now. Begin with a Basic.

SEVENTH MOTION — Fig. G

MEN:
· Raise right elbow as high as you can, to make a window for the woman to go through.
WOMEN:
· Duck as much as necessary, dropping you head slightly, and back out, under man's right arm, until you can stand.

ADVANCED • MOVE 6
PECKING

Men! Men! Wonderful MEN!

This is the first "lift" we're going to do. It's not hard, but use your common sense! If one of you is too big or small to do it, or if there's any reason you shouldn't lift or be lifted, DON'T EVEN TRY IT! A few tips: Once you start this move, forget the count. Just get it to be a smooth, continuous motion (which takes PRACTICE). When

you're done, pause, get the beat, and go into a Basic Step again. During the move, stay close to each other and hold on tight the whole time to avoid falling. Be careful not to bump heads.

TO START: Complete a basic step. Your first step out of the "Rock-Step" will be the first step of this move.

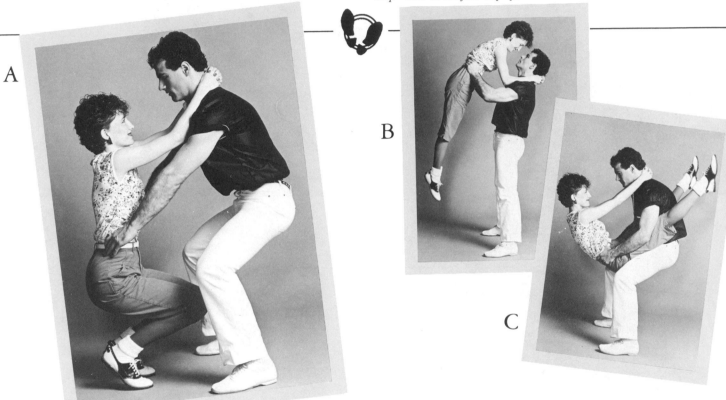

FIRST MOTION — Fig. A

MEN:
Plant your left foot about 12″ from your right foot, and put both hands on the woman's waist — thumb towards you, fingers on her back.

WOMEN:
Put your right foot next to your left foot (touching it), and bend your knees between the man's legs, as in a deep knee bend. Interlace your hands behind the man's neck.

AS YOUR FOOT LANDS:
· Put weight on balls of BOTH feet.
· Straighten your back and bend your arms.
· MEN: lean slightly forward and bend your knees.

SECOND MOTION — Figs. B & C
2 parts in one smooth movement

MEN:
· B) Bend your legs a little more, then forcefully straighten your arms and legs, lifting woman until her waist is higher than your shoulders.
· C) Bend knees and guide the woman down into position, straddling your waist.

WOMEN:
· B) Forcefully straighten your legs and push down on the man's shoulders with your forearms, propelling yourself straight up into the air.
· C) In air, spread your legs. As you descend, lean back and swing both legs forward, straddling the man's waist.
· Straighten your elbows as you land.

PECKING

D

E

THIRD MOTION — Fig. D

MEN AND WOMEN:
Lean forward, turning head to right, and touch left cheeks. Lean back (woman straightens her arms).
Repeat, turning head to left. Lean back (woman straightens her arms).
AS YOU LEAN:
MEN: Keep your knees bent, and your body stable.

· Support the woman with both your hands around her waist.
· **WOMEN:** Keep your legs straight, straddling the man's waist.
· Keep your weight on your hands, interlaced around man's neck.

FOURTH MOTION — Figs. B & E
2 parts in one smooth movement

MEN:
· B) Bend your legs a little more, then forcefully straighten your arms and legs, lifting the woman until her waist is higher than your shoulders.
· E) Keeping your back straight, bend your knees and support the woman's weight as she descends. Cushion her landing.
WOMEN:
· B) Push down forcefully with your forearms on the man's shoulders (keep your hands interlaced behind his neck),

throw your hips up and back, and propel yourself back into the air.
· E) In air, bring your feet together, straighten your legs and rest of your body, point your toes away from the man.
· Land softly on floor, bending at the ankles, knees, and hips to cushion your landing (feet together).
NOW GO BACK INTO OPEN POSITION AND WAIT UNTIL YOU PICK UP THE RHYTHM AGAIN. START DANCING BASIC STEP.

Jitterbug is for REAL He-Men

ADVANCED • MOVE 7
SIDE-CARS

This is easier than it looks — you don't have to be particularly strong if you do everything right. The rules for Pecking apply, though. GO BACK AND MASTER THAT MOVE BEFORE

YOU TRY THIS ONE. If you can do Pecking, you'll do fine with Sidecars. Remember to make it a smooth, continuous motion.

A

B

C

REVIEW PECKING, P. 82
BEFORE STARTING

FIRST MOTION — Fig. A

MEN:
· Step to left about 12″ with left foot. Bend knees, with weight evenly on both feet. Place hands on partner's hips, as in Pecking.

WOMEN:
· Assume same position as in First Motion in Pecking. Interlace fingers behind man's neck and do a deep knee-bend between his legs.

SECOND MOTION — Figs. B & C

· Both straighten legs forcefully.
· Woman pushes down on man's shoulders, man lifts her so her waist is above his shoulders.

WOMEN:
· Swing your legs to the right, onto man's left hip. You are essentially sitting on his left thigh.

MEN:
· As woman swings to your left, bend your knees and lean slightly right. This gently stops her motion without requiring great strength.
· NOTE: Key to this is not trying to stop woman's motion, but accommodating it. Let her "flow" into your hip, and provide thigh to support her.

The Jittermobile,
1952

"No, my next
dance isn't
taken . . ."

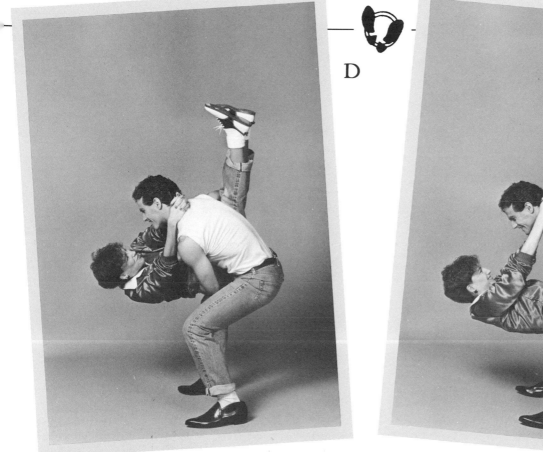

D

E

THIRD MOTION — Figs. B & D

MEN:
· Straighten legs and swing partner back in front of you, waist above your shoulders.

WOMEN:
· Swing your legs around and away from man as he brings you back in front.

Repeat Second Motion to opposite side (woman's left, man's right)

FOURTH MOTION — Figs. B & E

· Man brings woman back in front of him, and they do the Straddle (see Pecking).

SIDECARS ENDS THE SAME WAY THAT PECKING DOES. REFER TO PECKING FOR END OF MOVE.

ADVANCED • MOVE 8
THE SHOOT-THRU

Of course I believe you can do the "Shoot-Thru."

This move never fails to impress people, yet it's surprisingly easy. The key is getting the grip right. After you change hands, you might want to do a Basic while you arrange the grip. When you start the move, forget the rhythm and concentrate on getting a smooth, continuous motion. After you face each other at move's end, get into Open Position, wait for the beat, and go into a Basic.

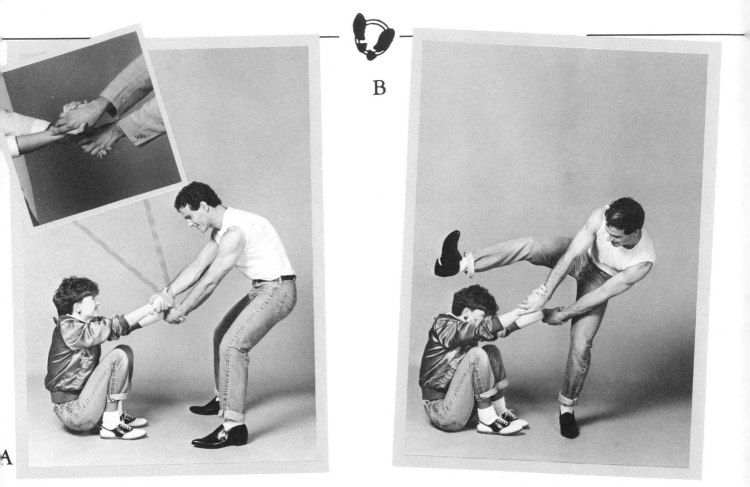

B

A

FIRST MOTION — Fig. A

- Couple gets into a cross-hand, wrist-to-wrist grip with right hands on top (see p. 52 and p. 72 for details). But with one important variation: Twist your right hands over so palms are facing right (left and right hands are now facing the same direction)
- Woman then sits, crouching so her behind almost touches the floor. Man stands with legs 12" apart, weight evenly on both feet, facing her.

SECOND MOTION — Fig. B

MEN:
- Swing your right leg over your partner's head, pivoting on left foot. Bend knees as foot lands.

WOMEN:
- Duck head slightly to avoid getting hit in head. As man's right foot lands, sit on floor. MAN AND WOMAN NOW FACE SAME DIRECTION, HOLDING HANDS THRU HIS LEGS, WRIST TO WRIST.

THE SHOOT-THRU

"He's been a new man since he learned to Jitterbug"

Great Balls of Fire

C

D

FOURTH MOTION — Fig. D

THIRD MOTION — Fig. C

MEN:
- Forcefully straighten your legs and pull your arms thru them, pulling UP. Pull woman thru.

WOMEN:
- Forcefully straighten your legs, pulling yourself thru man's legs.
- Duck your head as you shoot thru or he becomes a soprano.
- Swing thru.

MEN:
- When woman is thru your legs, pull up strongly with both arms, straightening your legs as you do. Be careful not to pull too hard. You are ASSISTING her to stand, not yanking her up.

WOMEN:
- When you are thru his legs, arch your back, straighten your legs, and pull up. As you stand, land softly on both feet, bending your knees to cushion them.
- Turn to face partner in open position.

AROUND THE BLOCK

This is the hardest move in the book. Not recommended for anyone but the best. Men: If you shouldn't be lifting, or if your partner is too heavy to try this with, don't do it! Women: You've got to trust your partner completely or you shouldn't try it. Start slow (although you can't do it too slowly). Forget the rhythm of the music while you're doing it — just get a smooth, steady motion. Be careful of the man's head.

I SURE LIKE MEN WITH GOOD-LOOKING HAIR!

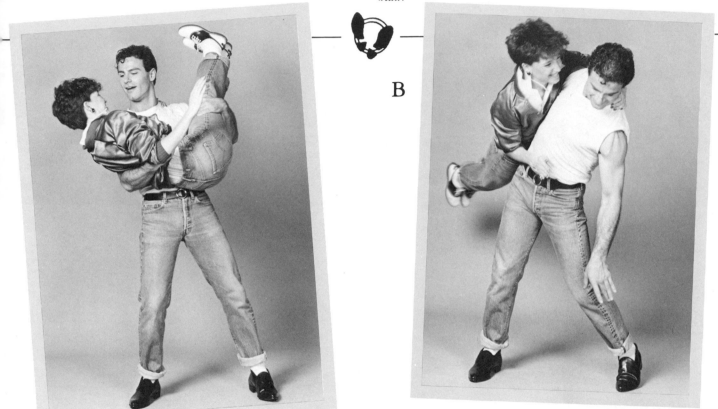

A

B

FIRST MOTION — Fig. A

- This move begins with a Basic Step in the Closed Position. As you do the "rock" in the "rock-step", moving away from each other, you bend your knees.

WOMEN:
Push strongly off the floor with your legs, and jump into the man's arms in a "cradle" position.

MEN:
- To assist the woman as she's she's leaving the floor, you straighten your knees and release her right hand with your left. Cup UNDER the woman's thighs to catch her in the "cradle" position.

SECOND MOTION — Fig. B

WOMEN:
- Forcefully swing your legs away from partner as he releases you.
- Push off his shoulder or or whatever's handy, with your right hand.
- Keep legs straight and together.
- Keep left hand around his neck, hand pressing down on his shoulder to control your speed.

MEN:
- Release left hand.
- Swing woman out and away from you, twisting to the right — this gives you both the necessary momentum to start the move.
- Lean slightly to the left and push up your right hip so partner will have something to support her as she goes around.

AROUND THE BLOCK

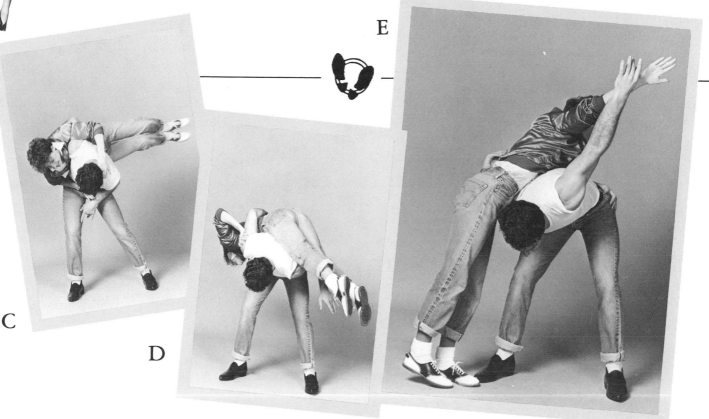

E

C

D

THIRD MOTION — Figs. C & D

WOMEN:

- Keep legs straight and together.
- As you swing across partner's right side, you'll turn slightly so your stomach lies flat on his back.
- Pivot on your stomach so your legs keep swinging around him (same momentum).
- Left hand comes off man's shoulder.

MEN:

- Bend over in a flat-back position — back is parallel to floor.
- Drop head — helps your back to stay flat, keeps it out of the way so it doesn't get kicked.
- Bend knees slightly to give you more support.
- Keep holding woman with right arm — now in back of you. This keeps her in place on your back.
- Allow partner to keep her momentum.

FOURTH MOTION — Fig. E

WOMEN:

- Keep spinning — stomach rotating on flat back — until you swing over his head and to his right shoulder.
- Keep legs out to avoid kicking him.
- At his right shoulder, slide your legs down over the shoulder, holding on to whatever's handy to keep balance and control.
- Land on feet smoothly, using your momentum to stand.

MEN:

- Still cupping her waist with your right arm, allow partner to continue her spin so that her legs travel over your head and to your right shoulder.
- When she reaches your shoulder, begin to raise your back and use your arm to facilitate her sliding down shoulder to land on feet smoothly.

Look at them Jitterbug!

ADVANCED ROUTINE

NOW BETTER THAN EVER!

Read through this Routine before you try it. Are you sure you can do everything in it? Don't try the Lifts if you're not able. This Routine incorporates a few moves from the Beginning and Intermediate Sections, and most of the Advanced Section. If you're *this far along, you should be able to substitute moves freely, using this as a starting point. Again, run through it without music first, very slowly, and then speed up according to your own abilities. If you can do it, then you've got a first-hand feel of the Joy of Jitterbugging.*

1. Intermediate Basic Step in One-Hand Lead

"Slow, slow, quick, quick"

TRANSITION: On "rock" of the "rock-step", man smoothly pulls woman as close to him as possible to make the hand-change behind her back easier. At end of "step", they are standing close, with man beginning to bring woman's hand behind her back.

2. Texas Tommy

"Slow, slow, quick, quick"

TRANSITION: Man holds out right hand as they "step". Woman places her left hand into his right.

3. Intermediate Basic Step in Open Position

"Slow, slow, quick, quick"

TRANSITION: On "rock" of "rock-step", man releases woman's right hand with his left, and stiffens his right arm so woman knows Legover is coming. On "step", she backs away (instead of moving forward) and bends her knees so their hands are low enough for man to swing his leg over. SAFETY FIRST ON THIS MOVE.

4. Legover

"Slow, slow, quick, quick"

TRANSITION: Couple "rock-steps" holding one hand (man's right, woman's left). On "step", man holds out his left hand and woman places her right hand into it.

5. Intermediate Basic Step in Open Position

"Slow, slow, quick, quick"

TRANSITION: On "step" of "rock-step", couple begins to pass, right side to right side, beginning to sweep arms up and out.

6. Shoulder Slide

"Slow, slow"

TRANSITION: DO NOT complete Shoulder Slide. As right hands slide down arms, grip at the wrists instead of sliding into partner's hand. On first "quick" count, which would normally begin the "rock-step", raise hands over your head in an arc, beginning the Fallbacks.

7. Fallbacks

"Move smoothly"

TRANSITION: At end of Fallbacks, couple is in Crossed-Hands position. Beginning a Basic Step in place, man ducks head as couple raises hands to place them behind his neck.

8. Standard Escape

"Slow, slow, quick, quick"

TRANSITION: Couple is in Open Position. On "step" of "rock-step", man assumes passing position (left side to left side), and begins making an arch in front of woman, by raising his left (her right) arm.

9. Underarm Turn

"Quick, quick, quick, quick"

TRANSITION: On "step" of "rock-step", man begins making a window to his right with his left (and woman's right) arm. Couple looks through it.

10. Reverse Underarm Turn with a Hand-Change

"Quick, quick, quick, quick"

TRANSITION: At "rock" of "rock-step", man has transferred woman's right hand into his left hand. At the "step", he holds out his left hand over their right hands, and she places her left hand into it.

11. Crossed Hands Position

TRANSITION: They begin to pass each other (right side to right side).

12. The Tunnel

"Move smoothly"

TRANSITION: As they come out of the Tunnel, both of her hands are in his right hand. Instead of letting go with one of her hands so they can return to a Basic Step, she places both her hands over his head, interlacing them behind his neck. As she does this, she bends her knees to get into Pecking or Sidecars position. He also assumes this position.

13. Pecking or Sidecars

"Move smoothly"

TRANSITION: At end of move (whichever you've done), as woman lands on her feet, she bends her knees to get into the Shoot-Thru position. Man spreads legs simultaneously, and they assume Shoot-Thru hand grip.

14. Shoot-Thru

"Move smoothly"

GREAT JITTERBUG RECORDS

Here are some songs and artists to guide you in picking out the best records to Jitterbug to. After listening to a few, you'll start to hear what distinguishes a good Jitterbug tune, and be able to pick out your own. I've included a little of each kind of music. Remember to start slow!

SLOW TUNES TO LEARN BY

Calendar Girl — Neil Sedaka (my favorite to teach by)
Stay — Maurice Williams and the Zodiacs
26 Miles — The Four Preps
Alley Oop — The Hollywood Argyles
The Wanderer — Dion
Isn't She Lovely — Stevie Wonder
Bobby's Girl — Marcie Blaine
Honey Don't — The Beatles (slightly faster)

'40s BIG BAND TUNES

If you pick the right band, you're sure to get some great dance music. Benny Goodman, Count Basie, Jimmie Lunceford, Glenn Miller, Duke Ellington, Harry James, and a newer band, Asleep At The Wheel are a few sure bets, but there are plenty more. Some sample songs:

In the Mood — Glenn Miller
String of Pearls — Glenn Miller
Boogie Woogie Bugle Boy — Andrews Sister
American Patrol — Glenn Miller
Woodchopper's Ball — Woody Herman
Route 66 — Will Bradley

GREAT JITTERBUG RECORDS

ROCK'N'ROLL OLDIES
(Just a sample of the thousands of great ones)

Johnny B. Goode — Chuck Berry
All Shook Up — Elvis Presley
Jailhouse Rock — Elvis Presley
Great Balls of Fire — Jerry Lee Lewis
Whole Lotta Shakin' Goin' On — Jerry Lee Lewis
Rave On — Buddy Holly
That'll Be the Day — Buddy Holly
Reelin' and Rockin' — Chuck Berry
Barbara Ann — Beach Boys
Rock Around the Clock — Bill Haley and the Comets
Bony Maronie — Larry Williams
Runaround Sue — Dion
Splish Splash — Bobby Darin
Good Golly Miss Molly — Little Richard
Reet Petite — Jackie Wilson
Finger Poppin' Time — Hank Ballard and the Midnighters
Blue Suede Shoes — Carl Perkins
Why Do Fools Fall in Love — Frankie Lymon and the Teenagers
Get A Job — The Silhouettes
Come Go With Me — The Del-Vikings
Sea Cruise — Frankie Ford
Be-Bop Baby — Ricky Nelson
Chantilly Lace — The Big Bopper

NEW ROCKERS
(A sample to show that they still make 'em like they used to)

Danny's All-Star Joint — Rickie Lee Jones
Rev It Up and Go — Stray Cats
Sexy and 17 — Stray Cats
If Sugar Was As Sweet As You — Rockpile
Rockin' Round NYC — Marshall Crenshaw
Tell Her About It — Billy Joel
Fishnet Stockings — Stray Cats
Working for a Living — Huey Lewis and the News
Fool Too Long — Rockpile
Border Radio — The Blasters
Rock This Town (very fast one) — Stray Cats
Bikini Wax — Killer Pussy
I Keep Gettin Paid the Same — Joe Ely
Rock'n'Roll Girl — Dave Collins and the Beat
Betty Lou's Got a New Pair of Shoes — Neil Young

HOW TO HAVE A
JITTERBUG PARTY

**TIME TO INVITE THE GANG OVER FOR A PARTY.
HERE ARE A FEW HINTS:**

PICK A THEME.

- **A Sock Hop.** In the '50s, school dances were held in gymnasiums. Since shoes would scuff the gym floor, dancers had to Jitterbug in their socks. Today, "sock hop" is synonymous with "'50s party". Everyone comes dressed as their favorite '50s character, wearing letter sweaters, rolled-up jeans, poodle skirts, etc. White socks are mandatory.
- **Greaser Party.** Be the Hood of your dreams. Grease your hair back. Get out those black fish-net stockings and black leather jackets. Start cracking that gum. Everybody comes as their favorite juvenile delinquent. Decorate with stolen hubcaps.
- **Prom Night.** You waited 4 years for the Senior Prom in high school. Now you can have one whenever you want. Dig up those funky old prom gowns and iridescent tuxedoes. Long gloves, corsages, high heels, and bee-hive hair-dos.
- **High School Reunion.** Everyone comes as their favorite '50s high school character. Teachers, jocks, cheerleaders, Nerds, and anyone else who caught your fancy way back when.
- **A '40s Party.** All Reet! Hep Cats in Zoot Suits. Cool Kittens with padded shoulders and stockings with seams — or baggy jeans and saddle shoes.
- **Pep Rally.** Come dressed in school colors and cheerleading outfits. Be prepared to show off your favorite high school cheers. Decorate with high school pennants.

DECORATIONS

- Use streamers and lots of balloons
- Draw pictures of instruments on poster board, cut them out, and post them around the room. Don't worry if you can't draw — the funkier, the better.
- Spread old magazines and high school yearbooks around the room.
- Put up a banner that says something like: "Welcome Class of '57", or "Go Tigers — Beat Riverdale!!"
- Put old album covers on the wall.

THE DANCE FLOOR

- If you've got a wood floor, you're all set. If you've got a carpet, get people to take their shoes off. And Jitterbug needs some room, so get everything out of the way.

MUSIC

- Make a tape of good Jitterbug tunes before the party (don't forget to mix in some slow songs!)
- Tell everyone to bring their favorite 45s.
- Get some Rock'n'Roll Anthologies, or Big Band albums.

HOW TO HAVE A
JITTERBUG PARTY

FOOD
- Go All-American. Hot dogs and hamburgers. Pizza and potato chips. Real Jitterbuggers don't eat quiche. And don't forget the dip.

PARTY DANCES
A "must" for any Jitterbug party. So bizarre they're really fun. Here are a few classics:
- **The Freeze Dance.** One person mans the record player, one is a judge. The person in charge of the record player periodically stops the music and shouts "Freeze". All dancers have to stop in whatever position they're in. The judge walks around and taps people out if they're moving, and they become judges, etc. Keeps going until the last couple is left.
- **Multiplication Dance.** One couple starts out dancing. Leader yells "Switch", and each member of the couple has to find another partner. Now there are four people dancing. Yell "Switch" again, and all four have to find new partners. This keeps going until the dance floor is full. Keep time between "switches" short or the crowd drifts away.
- **Matching Halves.** Cut some photos out of magazines and cut them in half (the more bizarre, the better). Separate top halves for women, bottom halves for men. Hand them out. Dancers have to find the person with the matching half and dance with him/her. Variations: use playing cards, riddles or jokes (men get the questions, women get the answers/punchlines), rhymes, etc.
- **Sock Hop Cinderella.** Put one of each woman's shoes in a pile in the middle of the floor. Each guy grabs a shoe and has to dance with its owner.
- **Balloon Stomp.** Every couple has a rubber band and a balloon with a number on it. One member of the couple attaches the balloon to his/her ankle with the rubber band. Then they start dancing. During the dance, you call out a number, and everyone stops to find out whose number it is. They resume dancing, with the whole crowd trying to stomp on their balloon and break it. When the balloon is busted, they're out. Keep going til there's only one couple left.
- **Flashlight Dance.** Turn out the lights, and at brief intervals, flash a flashlight on one of the couples dancing. They're eliminated. Keep going until there's only one couple left.

WRITE TO DR. JITTERBUG

• If you have a favorite move that you think ought to be included in future Jitterbug books, I'm all ears. In fact, if no one else suggests it, and I use it in my next Jitterbug epic, I'll pay you 25 smackeroos AND give you credit for it in the book!

• If you've got any suggestions about the moves or instructions, let me know.

• If some hip club owner is featuring my favorite dance, I want to know about it so I can send him or her my Official Jitterbug Seal of Approval! Hey, that's the least I can do! So send me that club's name and address.

• If you're interested in learning more about the Jitterbug, or pursuing you lessons with a "How To Jitterbug" videotape, send your name and address, and I'll notify you when it becomes available.

Write to: **Dr. Jitterbug**
Box 28
Englewood, NJ 07631